Transforming Your Life

A Step by Step Guidebook to Personal Success

By: Connor J. Pierce

Printed in Canada

First Printing, 2016

ISBN 978-0-9950092-4-0

Dead Canary Solutions
180 Lauder Avenue
Toronto, Ontario M6E 3H4
CANADA

www.deadcanarysolutions.com

www.transformingyourlifeguidebook.com

ACKNOWLEDGEMENTS

There have been many influences in my life, but none as strong or pervasive as that of my wife, Nancy. I was fortunate enough to meet the love of my life in high school, marry her a decade later and have two wonderful children with her. Life was not always easy but we have always reached for our dreams together, with each other's support, guidance, honesty, and love. Our children Logan and Riker bring joy into our lives on a daily basis and give even more reason for me to deliver the knowledge, wisdom and hope within this work, so that the world that they grow up in is in a better state than that in which we found it.

My mother Viki uprooted her life at an early age and travelled half way around the world in hopes of a better life for her family. She found a place in Canada, built a life despite many disadvantages and setbacks, and persevered. She has truly been an inspiration to me and I love her for that.

To the many mentors, teachers, friends, and loving family members that have consciously and subconsciously been invoked throughout the writing process, your wisdom and guidance have made a positive impact on my life and I am richer for knowing all of you.

And last but certainly not least, to you the reader who has chosen this book from a vast ocean of knowledge, I thank you for providing hope to me that in this complex and wonderful world in which we live, there is value in a single voice, hope in a single heart, wisdom in a single mind, and peace in a single soul. Your journey is my journey and I look forward to walking through it together.

Dedicated to the single transformative thought
that in execution changes our world
to bring light to darkness,
hope to the hopeless,
and wisdom to all.

Most of all for me, to my wife Nancy,
who is the most humble giant
to ever grace my life.
You have made me better every day
that I have had you in my life.

Table of Contents

PREFACE

We are being lied to every day. They come to us from different sources: television, radio, and internet ads; books; magazines; newspapers; people; corporations; and others. They claim to deliver happiness, knowledge, health, wealth, success, hope, and freedom. Every day, we are bombarded with an endless stream of products, services and information that claim to produce the answers to our every need and desire. These worthless LIES intended to dupe weak minded into giving away their hard earned time and money. The prey for these lies are the unthinking people of weak character that are cowardly willing to believe they can get something without working for it. With their heads in the clouds, they buy into the idea that these false idols can bring them all that they desire and save them from their troubles. So why do people buy into this crap? They don't know any better! We all have needs, wants, and dreams that we want fulfilled but most of us don't know how to create or achieve our own successes or build our own dreams, so we buy into the idea that these products, services, or things will help us achieve happiness. Through this book, you will learn everything you will need to know to achieve your own success and build your own dreams. There are no false idols here, so read on and get ready to learn, and apply the steps in this book to build your own dreams.

For most of my adult life, I have shied away from the idea of teaching. Despite being told over a long period of time and in many different forums both private and professional that I have a natural inclination toward delivering a message or information, I always discouraged the label of teacher. I think the reason for this is because I have a lot of respect for teaching as a profession and did not want to discount the amount of time and effort that members of the teaching profession laboriously devote to their field through formal study and painstaking, and often ill recognized, work in the field. Usurping this title was never an option for me.

I am a realist and an honest one at that, and I would not be the first to recognize that among the many sources of learning that I have experienced over my lifetime, the ones that have mattered the most in the grand scheme of things and which have led to the wealth of success and knowledge in my life, have not come from teachers or formal education as a whole for that matter. What I did figure out was that learning is an internal process that can only be controlled by my desire for knowledge, and for me I wanted to learn so that I can make my dreams come true and build the life that I wanted and deserved.

Within the pages of this book, you will find real knowledge and wisdom that has been refined for thousands of years to help those who understand it achieve greatness. These practical skills are within reach of all of us: young and old; educated and uneducated; rich or poor; man, woman or child. Everyone can benefit from incorporating even a fraction of this knowledge into their daily lives. No matter how difficult your personal situation might be, it is not too late to change the course of your life and attain personal happiness.

I don't have dreams so much anymore. Dreams are things to strive for that are out of reach. Knowing what I know now, the dreams I used to have are either present in my life now, are on their way to becoming a reality, or are goals for the future which I will tackle in due course. But what I will tell you is this, there are no secrets in this book, no hidden knowledge that may or may not be revealed by reading its pages. The knowledge set out here is written to be easy to understand and even easier to apply to your daily life to start you on the track to greatness. And even if your goal is not to achieve greatness, following this wisdom passed down from the ages will make your life easier, free up your time, and deliver more happiness than you can imagine.

You may ask yourself when picking up books that professes to deliver any life change or tangible results in your life, where is the proof? Producing a short list of celebrities, business people, and others of questionable provenance as proof of a successful program or body of knowledge is frankly not enough for me. The proof I offer to solidify in your mind that the content set out herein will deliver positive and life changing results to you is all around you. In every sidewalk, road and highway, in every electronic device and video game, in every car, plane and train, the proof lies waiting for you to open your eyes to it and use it in your life.

In the end, aside from knowing that applying the knowledge, lessons, exercises and guidance provided within the pages of this book will help you achieve any dream you have, this book is intended to provide hope. Hope for those that feel even a bit helpless or lost. Hope for those who want to achieve something but feel they do not know how. Hope for our children to show them that anything is possible. And hope for the beginning of a better world, one person at a time.

PART I

SIMPLE TRUTHS

Making dreams come true is within reach of all of us. This is a statement of fact, not just a belief of mine, because throughout my life I have seen dreams become reality and later on in my professional career I learned how this transformation takes place. The knowledge that will be shown to you in this book has been proven successful in the creation of marvelous empires, global change, masterpieces of construction, and innovations in technology that have transformed our world. But I will not just be describing these tools and techniques to you, I will personally be walking you through the steps you need to take to use them to achieve any goal and dream you can think of throughout your life. There is a long history of success backing the truth that this process represents the beginning, middle, and end of many of the greatest human achievements in history. I share this knowledge with you to transform your life so that you can begin making choices that will guide your life in the direction you want to go.

A Bit of Background

The Great Pyramids of Egypt, the Apollo moon landing, and the Three Gorges Dam in China have something in common with the cars on the street, the computer software we use daily to surf the internet, and the shoes you are wearing. All of these things started out as a single idea in someone's mind. Napoleon Hill once wrote that whatever the mind can conceive and believe, it can achieve. (Napoleon Hill, Think and Grow Rich, Chicago, Illinois: Combined Registry Company, 1937) Believing brings you half way toward achieving.

The thing is though, these adages and stories never actually tell us how to bring these ideas into reality, and without having a path to travel toward achievement, the ideas that we think of reserve themselves to the world of dreams. But when do dreams cross over into the world of reality? How do these unimaginable achievements of humankind evolve from an idea in someone's mind and travel through the dream state to enter the real world? This is what we will be exploring together on this journey.

Now I have read many "self-help" books over the last 30 years, and from those which at the time were thought to be enlightened and touted as "breakthroughs" in the media of the day, to the truly obscure programs and books that tried to shed light on achievement and the human condition, they always fell short of my expectations. Most were nothing more than a "Rah Rah Rah", you can do it … don't give up, story book of other people's achievements and old ideas that haven't really applied to the current condition in decades. Some were intended to be an introduction to the world of expensive seminars and private courses intended to show you how to attain personal success, from weight loss to financial success to a happier relationship and more.

Wow, that's a tall order for any book. Even so, the self-help section of any bookstore, library, or online book retailer is a virtual and veritable buffet of potential happiness, financial well-being, spirituality, personal and emotional development, or sexual prowess. The land of self-help is a super-highway where all roads lead to happiness and success. Unfortunately, for those who have read one or many self-help books, the reality is that the vast majority of these books lack substance, promote motivation as a skill, and fail to deliver on the promise of results. Motivation is not information, lighting a fire under a person's ass mostly just gets them burned, and the only thing they do is sell books, programs, systems, or expensive seminars. lies for the masses indeed. The main flaw, aside from the obvious lack of providing useful information, is that they do not take into account the unique individual reading the material.

People do not have the same: starting place; resources; access; information; knowledge; understanding; skills; networks; amount of money; or, strength of will.

Authors make assumptions to sell books, or they detail their own experiences and successes and think that everyone can do the same things to get the same results. It's like the world's fastest sprinter writing a book about running and saying anyone can run like they do, or a world champion golfer transposing their golf techniques into print leading the reader to think that at the conclusion of reading the book, their golf game will miraculously become world class. Well, this is what most self-help books do.

Not everyone can: afford healthy eating; exercise; afford education; buy a house to flip; renovate a house; start a business; buy needed tools, equipment or courses; enter the stock market; or, let go of past life experiences easily.

What is different with this book? I am not selling: hope; dreams; a predetermined package; someone else's experiences; or, crap.

I will be providing you with the means to help you develop your own ability to make your goals a reality. I am not selling you a map to where I have been. I will show you how to make your own map and follow it to wherever YOU want to go.

Like the big dreams of generations past such as placing a man on the moon, curing disease, creating peaceful political change, or building anything of lasting value, they all started as a dream in the mind of someone, and through determination, planning, hard work, and overcoming obstacles, those dreams have become a reality. This book is not just about big dreams though. It is about how you can transform your life into one of your own design.

This is what I intend to show you through this book. To turn any dream into a realistic project, develop a plan to make that dream a reality, and execute that plan to fulfil your dream. We will start with a small dream first to practice and then work to perfect your knowledge and skills. Once you have practiced what you have learned, you will be able apply your new skills to any dreams you may have, as often as you want. The skills and knowledge within these pages will provide you with a lifetime of support that you will be able to use over and over again to fulfil all your dreams. Once these skills are mastered, you will never buy into the lies and falsehoods which bombard you every single day, ever again!

This book is not meant to be a comprehensive compendium of project management knowledge, tools and techniques. There are literally hundreds of thousands of books, articles, journals, and other documentation on project management methodologies, tools and techniques. Some try to be comprehensive, others are basic, and yet others focus on highly specific aspects of project management that apply only to specific types of projects or fields of study.

What I have detailed here is the basic set of the most common and important tools, techniques, knowledge and understanding, to allow you to work on any project. Like a toolbox in your home may contain only the most essential tools that will handle 90% of the jobs you will need, unlike the auto mechanic or contractor toolbox that has every tool under the sun to meet their daily needs, you will be able to apply these skills to begin achieving any goals you may have starting today.

Why Self-Help Books Fail?

The premise of most self-help books is that you help yourself, through introspective reflection, self-determination, and independent effort. What a load of CRAP!

Most "Self-Help" books dump the responsibility of proving the worth of their theories and content squarely on YOU. You do all of the work, you sacrifice; you reap the rewards or suffer defeat … alone. This is why most people fail. They have been told they must bear this burden alone. That it is all about YOU changing yourself, your life, and the world around you. This approach is not reality. It goes against logic, against the whole idea of projects and project management, goes against our natural inclination as humans, and against any solid foundation of successful change. We are social creatures and doing anything alone in isolation has its limits. A single person trying to complete a project on their own is destined for failure, especially if they have a life to live, a job they need to perform in order to survive, and a family they need to support.

When people embark on "Life Change" and use the "Self-Help" book approach, they are more often than not overwhelmed at all the work and effort ahead, the sacrifice in time, money, friends, etc. They feel like they have to keep their journey and their struggle hidden for fear others will see them fail. This causes them to complete every aspect by themselves and have no time for anything else (in addition to their regular responsibilities).

The difficulty lies in:

1) People **don't trust themselves**, which is why they look into self-help books that make promises to help you change your life and fail to deliver anything of tangible value. Most self-help books would be classified as motivational (kick in the pants). This book does not kick you at all, but shows you real steps. At the end of this process, you will develop a deep trust in yourself and your ability to achieve your dreams.

2) People **lack the skills** to make changes. We all have different skill sets and come from varying backgrounds which will impact the way in which we can achieve any goal. Our capacity must grow to meet our needs and I will show you how to do this easily.

3) People see self-help work as "**supplementary**" to their current work schedule. This means they have to "sacrifice" personal time to work on changing the specific area of their life they want to change. You will quickly realize throughout the process I will guide you through, that the efficiencies gained and the concentrated effort from multiple sources, will save you time and effort, and thus balance out the work you put in. You will accomplish much more with a lot less time, and will create the breathing space you need to restructure your own life.

4) People do not meet the starting point or "**entry point**" for participation. For example:
   - Health
   - Money
   - Skills and knowledge
   - Motivation or commitment
   - Time
   - Patience (to see things through)
   - Personality

For example, a weight loss book may tell the reader to only eat seafood. Seafood is expensive. An average person can't afford to eat 5 meals a day with seafood at its core. This person cannot participate because they are not able to meet one of the core requirements for entry, which in this example is COST. Or if another person has an allergy to seafood, they also cannot participate because they are not able to meet one of the core requirements for entry, HEALTH.

Books about flipping homes to build wealth may tell the reader to buy a cheap home and renovate it to flip. A person with deep debt or bad credit may not be able to qualify to buy a house and may not be able to afford to renovate it. Also renovating requires a design sense to maximize the value (Return on Investment) of the renovation. So if a person lacks these skills, they may not get back what they spent in renovation costs on the flip. Also, tax implications may wipe out a large portion of the profit on a flip, which if you lack the knowledge, may hurt. There are many pitfalls with these making money quick schemes and everyone should be careful. I've seen it too many times, where people are selling "secrets" that are worthless, and the only thing they are really selling are books, courses or seminar seats. These people prey on the weak minded that are desperate and do not know any better. There are no free rides, and if you did have a secret system that was working to make you millions of dollars in your spare time, you would take that with you to the grave or pass it along within your family for as long as possible until it was also worthless. Then a dozen charlatans would pop up overnight with courses detailing what you have been doing … Lies, Lies, and more Lies … which does not work anymore. Whew, this cycle is exhausting!

We all have areas in our lives that we would like to change or fix. With enough desperation, the recurring question in our mind becomes … Can I change it? And the simple answer is YES! Whatever challenges you want to overcome or future you wish to design for yourself, you can build it, you can fix it, and you can do it now. But it has to start with certain promises that you need to make to yourself.

- To **value your time** above all else.
- To resolve to **identify and take swift action** to break free from elements that intend or want to continue taking your time, taking your money, and decaying your moral compass.
- To **consistently question** the systems of control around you.
- To focus on what you deem important in your life **above all else**.
- To **purge your life** of the negative influences that stand in your way to achieving what you set out to build.
- To be vigilant in your approach to change and take **ALL** of the steps outlined, as well as follow **ALL** the steps and principles that **YOU** set for your own life, from this point forward.
- You will **rebuild your life** the way you want it and never be controlled again.

Take some time to think about these promises, gage the impact they may have on your life, and whether you are ready to transform your life. When you are ready to internalize this promise, continue reading.

Having made these promises to yourself, you can then ask the question … How do I change it? … after which you can openly begin to understand that building something bigger than a single life needs to involve more than an individual life. A single person does not constitute a movement. Building and surrounding yourself with a fantastic team of people is how all great human achievements are realized. Working with a team of people, some of which have the same goals, is like rowing a boat. Row alone and when you stop, the boat stops. Row as a team and when you need a breather or need some support, other members of the team keep things going to support you until you can rejoin the effort. Those who have worked within a team environment know that doing anything else just doesn't make sense. I will show you how to build the greatest team you can in the following pages.

The Occupation Trap

Life is complicated. For most people in the developed world, the daily pattern of their lives becomes virtually automatic, but if we take a close look, we can see a vast range of interactions, fleeting moments and thoughts, constant movement from place to place with little thought of the complexity of this system we call life as a whole. We are too busy living in it to see, too consumed by our work, preparing for work, getting to work, coming home from work, trying to entertain ourselves to get our minds off of work, commiserating with our friends and loved ones about what happened today at work. You would think there would be a word for all of this work related activity … oh yeah, OCCUPATION.

Work, occupation, employment, a job, there are many words for it. The problem is that work has progressively begun to consume our lives to the point that our entire existence centers on it, our future is held hostage to it, we see our co-workers more than we see our families, and we pay other people to raise our children because we need to work. It is the way we have been conditioned from a young age and most of us feel trapped, helpless to change, fearful of the future, beaten down, and powerless. Since when did occupation become preoccupation?

Our saving grace was supposed to be technology. Sold as a way to free up our time and allow us to have more time to enjoy life, it has delivered many positive things to us, but has also had negative consequences. For example, when a worker left the office in the 1960s or early 1970s, their job was done for the day. Yes some would take work home with them but for the most part, their ability to communicate and collaborate with colleagues was over. Mobile phones, and then later smartphones, have since revolutionized the world of communication, allowing us to receive communications at any time of the day through voice, text, IM, and the like. As much as this has provided a positive for the world in terms of unprecedented access to information and people, it has also tethered us to our workplaces and allowed employers to take advantage on an unprecedented level. The first time you are asked by your supervisor, manager or boss, why you did not respond to an email at 11pm, you will have an explicit understanding of the expectation of constant availability. Computers have also increased our ability to complete work at an ever increasing rate compared to a mere few decades ago. The amount of work a person sitting in front of a computer can accomplish in a single day compared to what was possible 25 years ago is astonishing. But as much as technology has allowed us to perform tasks faster and more efficiently, communicate instantaneously, and deliver more work at an ever increasing rate, we have not been freed. The expectations of employers have grown to not only encompass all of the gains technology has offered to help mankind achieve freedom, but they have also encroached on our personal lives and time, to begin pushing the limits of what more can be taken from us. Five minutes here responding to a quick email, a 3 minute phone call to give direction to a colleague working late in the office, a once a month late night conference call overseas that you must be on, and more and more of our time is eroded along with our spirit.

The simple principle of payment of monies in exchange for work or value has become so distorted and so heavily manipulated by employers around the world that the line between personal life and work life no longer exists. It is now expected that when you begin working for a company, that they now own your current work, your future work, and your private life. You must make yourself available on demand. And the first time you mention that you cannot be available for whatever reason, you are out of town for a wedding or funeral, you have been sick and been unable to get out of bed, your spouse is giving birth to your first child, you will discover through the employers look or words of distain who owns your life.

Did any of us sign up for this? Did anyone see this coming? Have we all felt the effects of this pressure? And finally, what can we do about it now?

If any of these scenarios resonate with you and have led you to look for hope and a way to break free and recapture control over your life, I am glad you have picked up this book. Within these pages you fill find a path to freedom and a message of hope, but you will be the one who delivers your life back to your control and you will be the one that realizes the hope from within. I offer no secret knowledge to you, but will teach you the knowledge and wisdom that has been used and continues to be used every day by professionals around the world to deliver dreams.

Wake Up Call

The task of moving a mountain alone would take an individual a million years alone, whereas the same task would take a million people a year, and even less time and with fewer people using powerful tools, techniques, and modern construction technology.

When someone repeats the saying "Give a man a fish and he can eat for a day. Teach a man to fish and he can eat for a lifetime", the reality is that the context and application of this will change based on level of entitlement, perceived or real. What you will find is most people who have settled into their work life and are settled into their routines, do not want a teacher. They want a benefactor. Their will has been broken and they just want to be rescued. The funny thing about "Occupation" or as I like to call it, "Pre-occupation", is that it quietly consumes your life and your soul to the point that you do not even realize you are fully under its control. As it eats your time away, all free will is eroded until you know nothing else … and then you DIE. That is why we just want to be saved. We do not want to work to break this cycle that is the result of years of conditioning, through school, college or university, and every job you have ever worked. The training for your role as an employee has been taught to you your entire life. As difficult it may seem to unlearn and break free of its hold, all it takes is a single moment where you decide not to be held hostage to it any more. You will no longer be controlled by it. You will do whatever it takes for however long it takes to begin the process of breaking free of its control.

And don't dilute yourself into thinking that smart and wealthy people are immune to this system. You have for certain heard stories of high salary, seemingly successful people, being broke.

Large corporations that are essentially bankrupt. People living in mansions, driving expensive cars, travelling first class to exotic places … you think they own all that stuff? Don't kid yourself. Read "**Millionaire Next Door**" which is a statistics based study of who the actual millionaires in North America are and what characteristics they have. (Stanley, Thomas, and William Danko, The Millionaire Next Door, New York: Pocket Books, 1996.) The truly wealthy are regular people like you and me.

Teaching requires learning, which requires work, and when most people in developed countries come home from working their 8 hour work day, they've been conditioned by the media and other sources to fill the remainder of their day with entertainment, sports, winding down activities, and socializing to commiserate, among other distractions. The advertisers tell you that you "need" a vacation, you "need" a car, and you "need" this or that expensive high-tech thingamabob. Your choice is no longer considered. They are telling you what you need to buy or what to do. It is now a fact … you need this, you must buy this, you must do this. Even if you have no money, you need to get more credit to get it, and leverage your future for the NOW. WAKE UP!!

It is these distractions that eat up all available personal time and that keep employees and the masses "under control" and in servitude. They destroy free will and any chance of personal independence, independent thought, wealth, long term happiness, and freedom.

It sort of sneaks up on you later in life, at those "Where did the time go" moments where you reflect on your life, career, the world around you, and your progress toward anything of interest to you. It is these moments which should sound the alarm that your time is being stolen, that you are not in control but are being controlled, that should be your wake up call to act and break out of this routine.

As simple as this may seem, to most of us this moment will be a fleeting thought that will quickly disappear until another year, decade or lifetime has passed. And after all is said and done, for those stuck in this behavioral trap, regret, disappointment, depression, and hopelessness will settle in for the remainder of their days. The lucky ones will live in blissful ignorance of the life of wasted potential and "occupation". The root of which is to occupy your time to keep you enslaved to the system of control around you. In a very real sense, your life is being controlled and you are being monitored throughout your life by forces that want to keep you under control for their benefit.

- Banks
- Taxes
- Government
  - Health cards
  - Drivers licenses
  - Passports

- Corporations
- Credit and credit cards
- Insurance
- Utilities
- Laws
- Etc.

These bodies and systems have eroded your freedoms and deprived you of choices, and your future. Although this system exists all around and is difficult to totally break free from, every person still has "Free Will". To choose a direction that will lead them to freedom and happiness.

Now I am not advocating eliminating any or all of these institutions, after all I am in no way an Anarchist. What I am advocating is for each person to develop an awareness and knowledge of these systems, and these (and other) institutions, in order to slowly minimize or eliminate their negative effect on your life. I want each of you to think, question, and try interacting differently with these institutions and systems to see the possibilities. For example, how many stories have you heard of people being taken advantage of by being double billed for a product or service, yet most people trust that their credit card, utility bills, or tax bills are correct. They pay them regardless of the value and never question the accuracy. And if or when they do find that they have been double billed and raise this concern with the provider, they get pushback and delay and eventually have to fight for months to get a resolution or refund, under threat of a tainted credit report. Is it right to be taken advantage of? … Of course not! Do service and product providers take advantage? Of course they do. Will this ever change? … Probably not. Maybe you can't save the world from the vast degrees of daily injustices, but you can at least try to save your family and minimize these negative impacts on YOUR life.

Breaking free from this trap requires focus, burning conviction, a plan, resources, and your own system to build your new reality.

This is where project management knowledge can help. Project management provides a simple framework that helps a person break down a goal and develop a roadmap to achieving that goal in the most effective and efficient way possible.

The word "secret" is also used quite frequently within the world of Self-Help. As if the achievement of any level of success must come at the expense of a book, seminar, or DVD set which "teaches" you some novel new way of approaching the world that will change who you are and start magically attracting everything you desire in the absence of any work whatsoever.

Well I am happy to reiterate that there are no secrets, outdated stories, or breakthroughs in this book. By following the steps in this book, you will walk through the complete process of making your dreams a reality. Not only that, the steps laid out herein are repeatable so that you can continue to apply them to any and all the dreams you have throughout the rest of your life. I know that may seem like a tall order for any book, but you will discover as you complete these steps that your mindset will be forever changed to know that anything is truly possible, and that this path is the way to achieve your dreams. In fact, millions of people around the world use this knowledge and understanding daily to drive humanity forward, give us new technologies, build things that have never been done before, and take complex ideas and make them a reality.

Although this book is not intended to catalog, highlight or solve all the ills of the world, or combat the daily existential evils that surround us and that fight against anyone who tries to break free of their control, we must all develop our own insight into these bodies, systems, people, organizations, to become aware of their scope and impact on our lives and the challenges and risks they represent to achieving our goals so that we can plan to deal with them when they present themselves.

Why we do it?

What do we do it all for? I ponder this question as I look into my sleeping sons face. He is 9 years old, and is enjoying his early years of school, blissfully unaware of the day to day struggles of the adults living in this time. It is almost a decade after the (2007-2008) global financial meltdown, most countries have had austerity measures in place for years and have continued to tighten them over the past decade, and most people throughout the world have struggled throughout the meltdown. Our morality has been tested. Our resolve has been tested. Our will has been broken and we have been conditioned to accept the current reality as the only reality, to the point that we are desensitized to the life we are living, the control we have relinquished, and the masters that now control our fate. It is a David and Goliath story with us as David and many Goliaths including governments, banks and financial institutions, unscrupulous employers, and anyone else trying to take everything you have. They are all trying to take, take, take and distract you from your life through entertainment, sports, food, movies, and other measures that keep you preoccupied, to your self-imposed "escape", not through drugs or alcohol, but through your own broken mind, broken will, broken morality, and broken life.

Life shouldn't be this hard!

Everyone is different, has different goals, different aspirations, different dreams. You must throw down your shackles; become your own benefactor and start rebuilding your life to what YOU want it to be. Although this may seem like a mountain of work and effort, it is not a mountain to climb like you have been doing throughout your life, with more and more weight and responsibility and difficulty with each coming year. Today is the day you stop climbing up the mountain and start descending back to your basecamp. What I will show you along the way is how to make your life easier, make your journey more effective and efficient, gain momentum toward achieving your goal, and bring you home to the life you were intended to live. Happier, healthier, more financially secure … a life full of choice and freedom. This is all about to change right now.

I will first show you real techniques, processes, guidance, and examples that will walk you through reshaping your world, to take back what is rightfully yours; your time, your will, and your freedom. This book is not a feel good self-help book that supplies motivation and a proverbial kick-in-the-pants while providing no knowledge, substance, or process to help you. Now don't get me wrong, there is work involved and it is not an easy journey, but I can tell you that everyone who just begins this journey will begin to develop skills and knowledge that will provide positive and lasting results that will encourage them to continue. The work will get easier and easier the further you go and by the end of this process, your life will be forever changed into a life that YOU have chosen and built.

Remember, this is also not a typical self-help book that requires you to do all the work, tells you to devote hours and hours of additional time on top of your typical daily routine to see even minimal results or tell you to follow a path that someone else has developed and which has worked for them based on their personal experiences. This book is about YOU. You choose the path, you make the decisions, you design your journey, and you take yourself there.

This book intends to raise the curtain to the most powerful knowledge that has been in front of you all along. Enjoy the journey and I hope to see you on the other side. Walk with me.

FOCUS ON YOU

One day when my son was seven years old, he came to me crying at the end of the day. I asked him what was wrong and he said that a friend ruined his perfect day. He had just finished having a fun packed day with a play date at a friend's house, lots of video game play, outdoor games, and a nice dinner. It was a holiday long weekend and fireworks were going on in our neighborhood. The friend prevented my son from seeing the local fireworks, which made my son very upset, to the point where he came crying to me. I listened to him describe his perfect day and the final event that he thought ruined it. I told my son that his perfect day is not ruined because all of the fun things that happened on that day still happened and that the only way his day would be ruined is if he gave the power to ruin it, to someone else. As soon as you give the power to control your perspective to someone else, your day will be ruined, but as long as you are in control and you focus on all of the good things that have happened today, your day will never be ruined. I think this is good advice for any age and any person. Ultimately YOU are in control of your life and as long as you do not give someone else the power to influence your perspective, you can build any life you choose. Limits are what others impose on you, and if you choose to believe in those limits, then your choice has been stolen from right underneath your feet.

YOU are the most important element here, you have the power to decide the level you want to participate and the level you want to commit. What I am providing you with is a way for you to chart out and document a map to achieve goals that YOU set and the life that YOU want. Once the map is complete, I will walk through executing your plan to a successful result and locking in its gains so that you can move on to your next goal and eventually dream bigger and accomplish more.

I realize that everyone has different dynamics and elements to their lives, but one of the beautiful things about project management is that it is fully scalable from the most simple to the most complex projects, from small to large, from one project to many projects. It is a toolbox where you pick the specific tools you want to use and knowledge you want to apply to each unique project. Some tools you will use in one project and not another. Some techniques you will use often and may even incorporate into your daily life. You can start small and then add more ideas or goals as you get comfortable with using the tools.

To make this journey easier for you and to ensure you get the absolute most out of this book, I have included a series of Forms, Worksheets, and Templates that will help you capture each stage of this journey. These are not only added to the end of this book, but are available on the following website, **www.transformyourlifeguidebook.com**, for free download and use. As we progress through this book, these tools will be highlighted at the time of their intended use, through a specific boxed note with reference to the needed form, worksheet, or template displayed prominently in the dialogue of this book. I will also be adding to these useful tools as time goes by to provide additional support to you and the achievement of your goals, which will be added to future versions of this book, but again available for free download at the mentioned website. You can feel free to download, print and modify these tools in any way that will add value to your specific situation. If you are printing these forms, I suggest keeping all your materials in a binder so that you can add to and reference the progress in your journey. These are tools to help you and if there are any additional tools, applications, or technology you feel like using in addition to these, you should feel totally comfortable using any additional tools you feel are helpful to you.

Now before we begin our journey together, I must encourage anyone reading this book to do two simple steps to prepare. For some of you this will take only a few minutes, for others it may take days or even weeks. We are all different and I respect each and every one of your unique qualities and the unique life you have lived to arrive at this point. That said, let us take our first steps together right now to start on a path to happiness and success.

Journal Form

Print five copies of the Journal form and place it into your binder
to begin documenting your thoughts as we begin our journey
together. You can print more later if needed.

Forgive Yourself – The Past is the Past

We have all had successes and failures in our lives in varying measure and magnitude. This is part of being human. It is ingrained into our essence and will continue throughout this journey we are taking together. When you are working through this process, you will continue to experience both successes and failures. What you need to realize is that the management of a project is not a success or fail, win or lose proposition. It is like travelling on a road where you will experience many road blocks and failures. When you get to these points, that can never fully be planned for, you will use different tools to chart a route around the roadblock, or apply a different technique to bypass the obstacle to continue on your path to success. Plans that we develop together will be changed many times throughout your journey, but it is important for you to realize this is a natural process and a single failure will not stop you from achieving your goal. So for all past failures and future failures to come, forgive yourself. We are more than the sum of our failures. We will do better each time and when we come across a failure again, we will get better at forgiving ourselves and move on faster and better than before.

In your Journal write down any major failures in your life that have stuck in your mind to this day. Describe the cause of the failures, the impact that they have had on your life, and what you have learned as a result of the failure. After each described failure, write a few words to yourself detailing how you have forgiven yourself for the failure. This may be a new exercise for old failures, but it is an important way to put these situations in their right place in your own life history.

Focus on the NOW

Much of our days are used up by thoughts of the future or the past. We plan ahead for the weekends, holidays or vacation. We dwell on days gone by, people who we have met, happy times in our past. It is natural to think about the past and the future, but if we let the past and the future occupy our present, then we are not fully allowing ourselves to control our lives. Many people have fallen into a pattern or a daily routine that they feel helpless to change. The pattern may be a culmination of years of experiences and may feel comfortable to the point you might not even notice it is there. We wake up in the morning, prepare for the day by getting washed up and dressed, eat breakfast on the go, and head to our workplace. We work for a bit, accomplishing much or little, eat lunch with friends to commiserate, go back to work to close out the day, head home, wash up for dinner, eat alone or with family to reflect on our day and then unwind in front of the television or computer until bed time beckons.

Most people want to turn the world off at the end of the day, and those people rarely achieve their goals.

This pattern can last a lifetime, with a few additional relaxation days, vacation days, interspersed with the odd family gathering or party. And every now and again we ask ourselves, "Where has the time gone?" If you have ever asked yourself this question, you have fallen victim to the trap of OCCUPATION. Your time has been occupied by your work (occupation), your support system for your work (i.e. your pre and post work routine) and your efforts to get your minds off of your experiences at work (de-stressing, entertainment, commiserating, etc.). During this journey, I will provide you with help in recognizing and dealing with this trap, but the first step is realizing that your time is being occupied by other people so that they can benefit. So let us take the second step together and resolve ourselves to living in the NOW and begin to reclaim your happiness and build your future. You are not destined to relive your past and are not only a dreamer of your future. You are in full control of your life at every moment and can choose whatever path you wish.

Journal Form

In your Journal write down as many sources or forces in your life that are actively stealing your time away from what you want to be doing. For each source of the pre-occupation, describe how it is stealing more time from you that you wanted, roughly how much time it has stolen to date, and the impact this has had on your life. Beside each source, write down two to three ways that you can limit or destroy the stealing of your time and start using that recaptured time to live in and focus on the NOW.

COMMON KNOWLEDGE IS NOT THAT COMMON

Common knowledge is defined as something that is generally known by everyone or can be easily found through a number of sources. A few examples of common knowledge are the number of seasons there are, the number of days in a year, and the capital of the United States. Within our own lives, there is common knowledge specific to how we live, what we do, and who we are. They are truths and facts that define us and impact the way we interact with other people, expand or limit the scope of our lives, and allow or prevent us from taking opportunities. Some are secrets that we share with only ourselves and others we wear on our sleeves like a badge of honor. Whatever your common knowledge is, it should NEVER be ignored.

There is however a growing epidemic of willful or negligent disregard for personal common knowledge. The little voice inside your head is telling us not to worry about that, I don't want to think about that, I'll figure that out later. And as distractions and the occupation trap take away the time you had to figure things out, fewer and few options to learn, grow and break free present themselves until there is no time left and disaster is upon you.

Let this be your wake-up call that it is never too late to reflect on the truths in our lives and start or continue building an understanding of where we are, what we can do and what options are available to better ourselves and those around us that we care about. Now to capture all areas of our lives would require a book of its own, but I do want to cover what I consider the four core areas because these represent the vast majority of our daily lives and are essential factors in the general happiness we experience on a daily basis. The four areas are:

- Our Work Lives (Financial)
- Our Personal Lives (Free Time)
- Our Relationships (With others and with ourselves)
- Our Physical Wellbeing (Health)

Much of our lives stem from or are impacted by these four areas and developing an intimate knowledge of these areas helps us expand the options available to us exponentially. The key to the exercises that follow in the remainder of this part of the book is being totally truthful and honest with yourself. The following sections will walk you through gathering intimate knowledge of the four core areas in your life so that you know your own personal starting place on this journey. At the completion of these exercises, you will have greater visibility of where you are in relation to the life you imagined you would live, and using this knowledge through the remainder of this book, you will work on getting exactly what you dreamed of in your life.

Know Thyself

Most people think they know themselves implicitly but knowing yourself requires real introspection and honesty. Understanding your personal limits, triggers, desires, fears, and deepest darkest secrets requires that you stop and take stock of how your life has changed since the last time you reflected, and gage how you have grown as a person with all the new experiences that have influenced you. Getting reacquainted with yourself should be a regular scheduled event and not just an annual exercise performed in fear of a jolly old fat man in a red suit.

<u>Know Thyself Form</u>

Exercise

Take the time to write down your greatest fears, deepest darkest secrets, biggest personal failures, and any other things that you have lied about, cheated on, or done wrong.

Consider this your personal confession and initiation into a new life in which you will be totally honest with yourself on a daily basis. Take as much time as you need to write a complete list of all of your transgressions, fears, thoughts that you have not shared with anyone but yourself, until it is all on the form. Once you are finished your list, find a quiet place away from anyone or anything that may distract you, and review your list by reading it aloud. Feel the words as if they are coming from the emotions that generated them onto the page. After reading the last item on the list, take a few minutes to let them echo in your mind until their sound dissipates.

It is at this point that you will take all of the pages from the form and any additional pages you have added to it; go to your backyard, front lawn, barbeque, local park with camping facilities or anywhere else in the great outdoors. With a lighter or matches, light the pages on fire until they are entirely engulfed in flames and watch them burn until they are entirely gone. As you watch the pages burn, let all of the negativity and weight on your mind and soul burn with it until it is entirely lifted away, leaving you with a clean slate to begin rebuilding yourself with complete honesty and light.

Once the pages have been destroyed, make this solemn vow to yourself.

"I solemnly vow never to reflect on these negative events in my life again, and if these thoughts do come into my mind, I will prominently remember that those components of my life are dead, burned, buried and gone, to live no more in my mind, heart, and soul."

Financial Reality – Your Work Life

How would you categorize your work life? Successful? Challenging? Enjoyable? You like the people, but not the work part? Of all the feelings we have about work, the one that we can all agree is consistent is that work is "necessary". Work is the necessary task that supports what you REALLY want to do, or at least that is what most people think. Although work is necessary to supply you with a tangible currency at a rate based on the value you provide to the employer, somewhere along the way work has become an all-consuming monster that confuses, distracts, occupies, and monopolizes our time so that in the end the currency provided is just enough for subsistence living. Work has increasingly become a control mechanism where workers are enslaved both during work, outside of work, and tied to work in their minds, every day, all the time.

Now, anyone who claims that they can "save you" from this cycle of despair is selling you lies. Only one person can deliver your freedom … and that person is YOU. What I would like to help you do in the next few passages is firstly to demonstrate the level at which you are under control and held captive, and walk you through some exercises that will provide you with the direction and confidence you need to begin weaning yourself away from the unscrupulous occupation practices of employers today to manage your employment as a tool to manufacture your own freedom. Remember, the role of a business is to ensure its own survival and growth. Your rate of compensation is negotiated up front and is set at a value that is consistent with the ongoing survival of the business. Compensation is set at the beginning of an engagement, so it is not based on merit. I have seen many instances where employers treat both excellent and poor performing employees the same. Any additional effort the good employee puts in to doing a great job does not entitle them to anything more than what was negotiated at the beginning. And regular pay increases are determined by years of service, rewarding inertia instead of competence. It is no wonder young graduates and professionals entering the workforce become quickly disillusioned with this system and jump from company to company looking for a different experience, only to find more of the same.

Different Income Types

Differentiating between different forms of income will first help you understand your existing financial state, and secondly open your mind up to other possible forms of income you may not have thought about as options in your life. As I guide you through these definitions, think about all of the different possibilities of adding different forms of income into your life.

> **Employment Income** – is an arrangement made by you and your employer, or client, for compensation on an hourly basis or volume of work.
>
> **Active (Earned) Income** – is money that is generated through the operation of an active business, consulting, or any other activity where time in compensated directly with money.
>
> **Passive Income** – is money that is generated through an investment such as real estate or interest bearing instruments. This could also include the sale or licensing of intellectual property, or any form of business where you continue to benefit from the effort of others after you have setup the business or system.
>
> **Investment Income** – is income that is generated through the sale of an investment at a higher price than it was bought (capital gain). This could include trading in stocks, bonds, mutual funds or other financial instruments, buying or selling real property and/or other assets for profit.

A lot of people dream of an ever expanding level of income to the point that they can afford the necessities and excesses that abound around them in the limitless bombardment of advertiser messaging. As fast as you can make it, you can spend it. This is the true underlying message. Income should be looked at as a tool, and if used wisely, can set the stage for prosperity in many forms. Let us take a look together at the buying power of your existing income and the influences that affect how much of it you keep.

Retirement Calculation

People hope that over time and through education, hard work, and perseverance, the value of their work can exceed what they spend now, so that the surplus can be banked for the future. This is the basis of savings for their retirement years, vacations, and life enjoyment activities. A single person trying to multiply and bank value like this is not effective.

For example:

If a person was to make on average $25.00 per hour and begins working at age 25 (after university or college) until retirement, we can forecast the future earnings of that person as follows …

Years from age 25 to 65 = 40 years

Average wage = $25.00 per hour

Hours worked = 8 hours per day

40 hours per week

2080 hours per year = $52,000 per year (before tax)

Total wages earned over their working life = $2,080,000

Minus taxes at a rate of 30% ($624,000) = $1,456,000

Minus the cost of a modest home ($300,000), doubled to account for the interest on a mortgage amortized over 25 years ($600,000 total) = $856,000

Minus a modest vacation of $1,000 annually ($40,000 total) = $816,000

The cost of a family - $5,000 per year, per child from 0-18 years old (one child = $90,000)

Minus the cost of ONE child = $726,000

If the person continues living the same lifestyle at a rate of $52,000 per year, the total savings they have remaining of $726,000 would last them approximately 13 years.

$$(\$726,000 / \$52,000) = 13 \text{ years}$$

This value would support the person for 13 years past the age of retirement or in this example, until the age of 78 given a retirement age of 65.

To be financially secure, you must develop systems that multiply effort and value so that you can continue to benefit from ongoing value after a project is complete or a system is created.

Now I know what you are thinking, for those higher income earners, this does not necessarily apply to you because you earn much more than $25.00 per hour. The thing about these calculations is that they scale to any income level. To put this into perspective, a higher income earner may choose a larger home costing more money and with a larger mortgage, take more lavish vacations more frequently than once a year, pay more taxes, buy more pretty things and toys for themselves, etc. Basically, people scale their lifestyle to their income level. The life they lead, the things they do, and the things they buy would scale to the same level, to arrive roughly in the same place within the same timeframe.

In this basic scenario, I have tried to keep it simple, only taking into account essential factors to arrive at the rough 13 years of banked income value in the example. The thing is, all other aspects of ones' life erode those remaining years; every meal, every movie, utility costs, medical costs and medicine they buy, furniture, transit, cars, gas, insurance, clothes, and the list goes on and on. Each additional expense taking away any remaining savings and years of support you need to survive in elderly years. In the vast majority of cases, the final number at retirement is in large negative numbers, which means that with no income to sustain a person in retirement, they are dependent on their children or the State to support them in old age. This is the legacy left behind for a life unplanned and unprepared. A burden on future generations.

Retirement Calculation Template

Exercise

Using the **Retirement Calculation** template provided, insert your values representing your own rate of pay, taxes, expenses and other information. Be as detailed as you can and see how the numbers break down for you in the end.

Employment Encroachment

How much time does your work consume in your private time? Emails looked at during private time, work being brought home, the work tether (phone, text, email – mobile device), the shaming of employees that do not devote every waking hour to their work. Can you take a vacation without the expectation of work being complete in your private time before you return, or even worse, work to be completed during your vacation? Are there underlings lined up behind you more than willing to devote all of their time to their work, who would make you look bad if you did not do the same ... or who your employer thinks or says are more than willing and capable of replacing you should the need arise?

Work life used to be easy to separate from private life prior to global communications and the internet, but employers have always been keen to extract the most value from their employees at the most minimal cost. In today's interconnected world, that means an expectation of availability and eagerness to work on demand. Most people do not even realize the amount of time devoted to their work outside of their regular work hours, because regular work hours have been superseded by "**all other duties as assigned**". When you agree to that, your life is gone. And for those of you "promoted" to even the lowest level of management, seemingly in title only, which is code for the same level of employer ownership without the need to pay you for overtime. Now not every company is the same, I'll give them that, but in this increasingly competitive business environment the larger the organization gets, the greater the tendency to exploit their employees time.

Employment Encroachment Worksheet

Exercise

As an exercise, complete the worksheet for a period of one week, in which you will keep track of every instance that you have completed any form of work for your employer outside of your regularly defined working hours. Every phone call, conference call, email, overtime hour at home, the office or elsewhere, and the like, should be noted along with the amount of time you devoted to completing the task. Also, note every time you thought about something work related in the worksheet. For emails, a quick tip is for you to look at your sent box at the end of the week and note every email written or sent after hours. You could also CC yourself on after hours emails and file them in a folder for the end of the week tally. At the completion of your full 7 day week exercise, add up all the time spent on activities completed after hours and review the outcome. If you have zero hours noted, you should feel ecstatic to know you are the envy of the remaining 95% of the global population. If you do have time logged, calculate the lost wages attributed to that additional time so that you know the amount of "charity" work you are providing to your employer. This exercise is designed to identify and quantify the amount of employer encroachment in your current work life, and let you begin to choose a direction based on this information.

After you have completed the exercise you may get the feeling that your employer is taking advantage, and in some instances you may be right, but understand that the goal of this book is not to have employees develop a distain for employers. There are good employers and not so good employers, and it is a sincere hope of mine that employers look to the knowledge within this book to empower and support their employees. I frequently provide guidance to corporations and advise that a key driver for ongoing business success is having happy and motivated people participating in any workplace, as this is an extremely valuable commodity in any industry, and supporting and empowering employee goals in their professional and personal lives should be the goal of every employer. It builds a strong workforce, sparks innovation, enhances communication, and promotes teamwork, creativity and loyalty. The relationship between employer and employee can be so much more, and I will expand on this theme later in this book.

Taxes

For employees, taxes are deducted at their source by the employer (source deductions), right off of your paycheck and remitted to the tax authorities at regular intervals, so that tax man has his hands on your money even before you see any of it. Not only that, your employer can use the money that has been held back for future remittance, for whatever period of time between the dates when it is deducted until the date is it remitted. A smart employer can earn additional profit by investing with this pool of money … your money … while they are waiting to remit it to the tax authorities. As an employee, everyone gets paid before you see any of your hard earned money. Pension Plans, Employment Insurance, Federal, Provincial, and State taxes are taken from your pay cheque even before it is given to you. You cannot use that money at all. You can only use what is left over after everyone else has taken their share.

This is specifically why business gurus, financial advisors, and people who have experienced both sides of the coin will tell you that to get ahead, you need to start your own business. Owning and running your own business is not easy however and you need to make sure you have a good accountant and lawyer to advise you. Typically, sole proprietorships can be started up at minimal cost, however you are at greater risk personally if something goes wrong. Incorporation, Partnerships and Limited Liability Corporations (LLCs) can now be easily registered on the internet for a few hundred dollars, but again there are tradeoffs. Accounting fees for corporations are substantially higher than personal filings and the tax reporting requirements are much more strict by comparison.

So what is the benefit of starting your own business? Access to **pre-tax dollars** is the simple answer. Let's go back to the pay cheque of the employee. Their buying power is greatly reduced when they only have access to their money, after all source deductions have been taken, using **after-tax dollars**. They cannot buy as much and they have to pay additional sales taxes on goods that they purchase with their money. Businesses receive money from their clients or customers and have full access to spend that money on things (expenses) related to the running of the business. They only pay taxes on what is left over at the end of the year. Also, when they buy something that has sales taxes applied, the business will get a refund of those taxes when they file their tax returns. Let's see if I can illustrate these facts by using an example.

Scenario 1:

An employee named Joe gets paid $15 per hour as a cook at a fast food chain for a 40 hour work week. In one month, he earns $2,400.00. With a personal income tax rate of 15%, pension of 5% and Employment insurance rate of 1.5%, he will have $516.00 taken from his pay cheque before he sees it, leaving him with $1,884.00 to spend. He pays $700 for rent each month, $300.00 on groceries, $200.00 on transportation to and from work, and the remainder on lunches at work, dinner with friends, and entertainment. The rent cannot be claimed as an expense. Groceries, lunches, dinners, transit costs and entertainment, have sales taxes applied at a rate of 10% which he will not able to take advantage of. At the end of the month, his buying power looks like this:

$2,400.00 (Joes wage) - $516.00 (source deductions) = $1,884.00

$300.00 (Groceries)
$200.00 (Transportation)
+ $684.00 (Work Lunches, Dinners, Entertainment)

$1,184.00 - $118.40 (10% sales tax)   (Note: $1,065.60 (what is really available for
                                        Groceries, Lunches, Dinners and Entertainment)
- $700.00 (rent)

$0.00   (This is the definition of living pay check to pay check)

Joe's buying power this month is the money he has access to spend, which in this case is:

$1,884.00 (wage after source deductions) - $118.40 (Sales taxes) = $1,765.60

Total Taxes paid by Joe is $516.00 + $118.40 = $634.40 for an effective tax rate of 26.43%.

Scenario 2:

Sally owns her own consulting business and uses her computer graphics skills to serve her clients. Her compensation fluctuates based on how hard she tries to recruit new business, but this month she has collected $2,400.00 in payments from her existing clients (the same amount as Joe in Scenario 1). She also averages 40 hours a week. Her corporate tax rate is also 15%, pension contribution is 5%, and employment insurance is 1.5%. She also pays $700 for rent each month, $300.00 on groceries, $200.00 on transportation to and from her clients, and the remainder on business lunches and dinners with clients, and business entertainment. The groceries, lunches, dinners, transit costs and entertainment, have sales taxes applied at a rate of 10%.

Sally has full access to the $2,400.00 to spend in her business. One third of her apartment is being used for her business, which entitles her to deduct $233.33 as an office expense against her income.

At the end of the month, Sally's buying power looks like this:

$2,400.00 (Sally's earnings are not subject to source deductions)

    $100.00 (Groceries – Minimal because she frequently has lunches and dinners on the go)
    $200.00 (Business Transportation)
+ $884.00 (Lunches, Dinners, & Entertainment with clients - $200 shifted from Groceries)

    $1,184.00 - $118.40 (10% sales tax)   (Note: $1,065.60 (what is really available for
                                                     Groceries, Lunches, Dinners and Entertainment)
    - $700.00 (rent)
    $516.00   (This money could be spent on business related items. If fully spent there would be a minimal tax position at the end of this month. i.e. personal income tax would only be applied to what Sally has spent on personal products like Groceries and 2/3 of her rent)

Sally's buying power this month is the full $2,400.00 as there are no source deductions to prevent its use.

    Tax Deductions include:
    $200.00 - Business transportation
    $884.00 - Business Meals and Entertainment
    $233.33 - 1/3 of the value of her rent
    $118.40 - Sales taxes
    Any other items she has purchased for her business.

    Taxes paid by Sally include:
    Sales tax on her groceries = $100.00 x 10% = $10
    Income tax on what she has spent personally:
            2/3 of her rent = $466.66 x 15% = $69.99

Total Taxes paid by Sally is $10.00 + $69.99 = $79.99 for an effective tax rate of 3.33%.

<u>Taxes Worksheet</u>

Exercise

Whether you are employed, unemployed, self-employed, run your own business or have another form of income, using the worksheet provided, calculate your own buying power based on the criteria outlined. Should there be additional information you would like to add, you can complete the additional information section provided for in the worksheet. At the completion of the exercise, jot down some basic notes about what you would change in light of the information provided that might increase your buying power in the future.

Fruits of Your Labor

The two scenarios in the section on Taxes above highlight the difference in buying power between an employee and a person that runs their own business. There is a significant advantage provided to those people who run their own businesses because they have full access to use the money they collect for activities related to the functioning of their business. Business lunches, business clothing, health club memberships, haircuts, manicures and pedicures, make-up, cars, computer equipment, and the list of items that can be fully or partially claimed as a business expense goes on and on. Also, any taxes you paid on business expenses are refunded to you at the end of the tax year.

As you use the funds you receive, for business related activities, the value of these items or services you buy are deducted from the business income. At the end of the tax term, you still pay personal taxes, however it is only paid on what is left over in cash and on what was paid out for non-business related items, such as the remaining 2/3 of Sally's rent. In the end, Sally has much more buying power to use day to day than Joe does, and although she pays the same tax rate of 15%, the actual taxes paid out is much less based on her low income after business related expenses.

Fruits of Your Labor Worksheet

Exercise

Again using the worksheet provided, write down all the forms of tax you pay annually, daily, on sales, property, investments, business, or any other form of tax. You will calculate this first by percentage to derive your total tax rate and then work to highlight how much or your income in all its forms is eaten away in taxes.

Taking Control of Your Financial Life

Generating income, keeping income, and getting the most use out of income is even more challenging today than at any other point in time. So many factors, influences, and forces surround us with the sole intent of bleeding all our hard earned income that we do not have enough fingers to plug the leaky dam. There are many ways to start getting help and support for setting your financial house in order, but a few simple places to start include the following:

- Consolidating Debt and pay it off
- Reduce the number of credit cards you have, and eliminating all department store cards
- Exploring Multiple Streams of Income – meaning the generation of income from a variety of sources from the income categories outlined
- Increasing your credit score so that you can qualify for more low interest credit
- Cutting your taxes by consulting an expert or restructuring your income streams to lower your tax exposure
- Look for savings in your current lifestyle
- Develop and follow a budget that works for you
- Based on the amount of additional work you calculated in the previous exercise on employment encroachment, ask for a raise to account for the lost value you are providing

The list of ways you can adjust your life to be more in control of your work and financial life is endless. In fact, people at every income level struggle with and work toward similar goals, the only difference being scale. Reach out and talk to people, do some independent research and actively look for ways to work within your current situation to slowly and consistently make adjustments that will put you on the right track. As you develop an awareness of your specific situation, take note of changes you would like to make and incorporate a plan for change while working through the remainder of this book.

Free Time – Your Personal Life

Let me first be quite clear about one thing … the world does not owe you anything, the universe does not owe you anything, your parents definitely do not owe you anything (once you become an adult), and for sure your employer does not owe you anything. Nobody owes anything to anyone. Some people may think they are entitled to a stake in the future or some opportunities that should not be available to others based on a variety of personal or professional experiences, or that they should be given a pass based on the actions or struggles of generations past, however the universe gives what it gives with no regard to who any one single individual is. The sooner everyone takes stock of this reality, it becomes plain and simple that it lies within us to create value in our own lives, not the wealth of our parents, not the color of our skin or to whom we were born, and not the money in this week's lottery. The daily frustration that comes from a life in waiting eats away at happiness and time you could be building your dreams. Hoping for some form of reparations for the past or inheritance from parents at the end of their lives is not living, but living in an unrealistic dream world. In the end when no silver bullet, golden parachute or saving grace reveals itself, and when all the value in the estates of your parents are left to the cat, you most certainly on reflection will agree that the time wasted in waiting could have been better spent. In the previous sections talking about this journey being all about YOU, self-forgiveness for any past failures and focusing on the NOW, I highlighted these specific factors because these are the keys to changing your perspective with simple truths that apply to all of us. And when you realize that you and other people who are extremely successful at what they do are essentially the same, you become more open to the reality that YOU are also destined for greatness.

When working through the exercises in this book and developing your own unique plan to achieve goals that are important to you, it will become crystal clear that your plan, your focus, and your journey toward achieving the outcome of your plan will force your life to realign itself. It will appear to an outsider looking in, that YOU are the lucky one, YOU are destined for greatness, that things are looking up and going your way. So when your friends and relatives say to you, "you are so lucky" to have what you have or do what you do, without seeing the hard work behind the scenes, try to ignore the ill placed sentiment and just be thankful they noticed. You will come to the realization at some point that most people do not care about the hard work needed to achieve something, they just care about getting that something handed to them by some miracle or sublime twist of fate. They "dream" for things that they see as unreachable for them because all of those things they see as fantasies. You at this point should know deep down in your heart that you will make your dreams come true, you will forge your own path and you will never look back to the fantasy land you are leaving behind. Every challenge you face head on and overcome will fall to the wayside and will become easier the more you tackle, and your life will become this dream making machine that will transform the world you live in and the world of possibilities in your mind. It will be at this point in your understanding that you will come to the realization that there is no such thing as entitlement. Your connection to the past and to the future will be defined by your focus on what really matters to you and the universe will respond equally to all who challenge it. And those people who persevere, keep their focus and use all tools available to them to challenge the universe will achieve their dreams and be given the opportunity to dream bigger. And the impact of an individual, a group of individuals or even a large group of people on your life, however negative you see it at the time, or hurtful, or destructive, are insignificant to the power you hold within yourself to choose a better path. Easier now than at any other point in history is your ability and access to connect with people all around the world with similar goals, dreams, and thoughts. You have a support system waiting for you, you have friends waiting for you who will not judge and will not tear you down but build you up and support you in your journey. So if someone tries to make you feel bad, tries to hurt you or tries to put you down, just know that there are over 7 billion other people on this tiny planet willing to be your friend.

Finding the Time

Everyone wishes at some point for a bit more time in the day. We explored how your time can easily be eaten away on seemingly small tasks that are performed almost as an automatic reflex, but now we will take a closer look at your days with a specific goal in mind … to find you the time you need to work on making the changes you want to your life. As I mentioned earlier, most self-help books tell to find the time to do what they want you to, without telling you how to "find" this imaginary time, forcing you to add their work onto your already overflowing plate.

In this exercise, you will find the time in your schedule to devote to your life changing activities without adding any more time to your day. So let's do the seemingly impossible task of creating more time.

<u>Finding the Time Template</u>

Exercise

Using the template provided, document your activities during a 7 day week. There is a sample exercise completed for your reference below. Once you have completed the template, describing the activity, start and end times, duration, category and priority, highlight only the Medium and Low priority activities.

This is an example of what a completed template for this exercise might look like this:

Day	Time	Duration	Activity	Category	Priority
Monday	6:30am	15 mins	Wake up	Necessity	High
	6:45am	30 mins	Eat breakfast	Health	High
	7:15am	45 mins	Shower and get dressed for work	Hygiene	Medium

	8:00am	1 hour	Leave and travel to work	Travel	High
	12:00pm	1 hour	Lunch with co-worker	Social	Low
…	…	…	…	…	…
Tuesday	6:00pm	1 hr 30 mins	Pottery class	Hobby	Low
…	…	…	…	…	…
Saturday	11am	4 hours	Movie double feature	Entertainment	Low
Sunday	9am	2 hours	Church	Religion	Medium

For the Medium priority activities, look for ways to either have someone else help you perform the activity, delegate the activity to someone else entirely, or for you to perform that activity more efficiently through better scheduling, grouping, or any other possible ways of completing the activity faster.. For the Low priority activities, first decide if they can be eliminated entirely, and secondly, explore ways to transfer responsibility for these activities to someone else. It might not always be possible to scale back our responsibilities, but reviewing our schedules with specific focus on finding useful amounts of time almost always bears fruit. At the end of the exercise, document the specific times you have carved out of your schedule and commit to using this time, and ONLY, this time to complete the work contained within this book. Remember, your focus is long term so make this as repeatable and regular as possible so that you develop a habit of using the new found time for YOU. Look for blocks of at least 30 minutes of time so that you can shift your focus and complete enough work to continue your forward momentum.

Shared Effort

As much as we know that, within a business or work environment, working in teams and delegating work to others saves time, increases efficiency and productivity, and produces better long term outcomes, all of that seems to go out the window when your brain shuts down at the end of the work day. The lack of teamwork and delegation of work to others who are capable of helping, in our private lives, is one of the key reasons why most self-help books are misguided. Everyone is a potential resource to help not only in the pursuit of your goals and dreams, but in your everyday life. The following exercise is designed to get you back in touch with the idea of shared effort, apply it in a simple sense, and help you calculate the general savings in time which can later be applied to a cost, to demonstrate value during any work you are doing. Once you master this concept, applying it in your daily life will free up a lot of time for you to focus on what is important in your life.

<u>Shared Effort Template</u>

Exercise

Choose an activity that you perform on a regular basis that is typically completed on your own, and time how long you take (duration) to complete the activity. A couple of examples may be folding laundry, grocery shopping, or prepping and cooking food in advance for your busy work week. Once you have timed how long it took you to complete the activity on your own, log the activity and time in the template. Before completing the same activity the next time, ask one family member, friend, roommate, or any other person to help you perform the task. Once you have provided them with brief instruction on how to complete the task and what you are looking for as a final outcome, time how long completing the activity took with help. Once you have the second time, log it next to your first time and calculate how much time, if any, you saved in the performance of the activity by sharing the effort with another person. This saved time represents time that you have recaptured in your life. Feel free to apply this to a variety of activities in your daily life and gage the difference and additional benefit available by splitting your effort.

Applying this knowledge to a business or your work environment can be just as effective as application in your private life. The difference is in the determination of gained value. For example, this technique of sharing effort is frequently applied within the world of computer programming where a highly paid employee such as a senior software developer is teamed with an administrative helper that is tasked with low level activities such as documentation. By doing this, the expensive resources' time is then solely focused on specialized activities which only they are capable of performing, while menial tasks that anyone is capable of performing are delegated to a lower cost resource. This arrangement allows the Senior Developer to be effective and retain focus, and conserves the value of their time for the best outcomes.

Sharing effort can be seen as a time multiplier in that more work is being completed in a shorter amount of time. Condensing the time it takes to do work by adding resources is an important concept that can be applied in many ways, but here you want to focus on how it can be applied to your own life to free up additional time. Try it out in a few different scenarios and log the results in your template for reference.

Relationships – The people in your life and your relationship with yourself

We are all naturally designed to be social creatures. It is hard coded into our DNA. Talking to people, making friends, sharing our experiences with others and caring about the welfare of other people is as natural and automatic as breathing for us … if we did not let our brains get in the way. Brains have a funny way of doing that after years of training. Preconceived notions, the messages we receive from all around us seemingly from every source we encounter, schools, churches, news, advertising, friends, foes, they are all absorbed, filtered and applied to our brains to shape our thoughts and experiences. With all the influencers trying to have access to our brains to sell products, promote their self-interests, and capture our attention for their own benefit, what was a natural function of our daily lives has now become a new model of Capitalism … Social Capitalism. Social activities have been replaced by social media however the media component is really the master in this relationship. For every natural social interaction you have in a given day, whether it be in person, on the phone or online, there are thousands of messages trying to shift your attention away from everything else and focus on the newest latest product to buy, service to use, app to download, news story to follow, or any number of other distractions to steal your valuable time away. This relationship has caused staggering increases in rates of anxiety disorders to the point that we cannot even imagine being "unplugged".

Human beings are fundamentally adaptable organisms that can change to survive, however evolution of this type takes time. What has been thrust upon us through the constant bombardment of media, technology and progress is wonderful yet our ability to adapt to that in a short period of time has been a struggle for many. In as much as we are now capable of doing from the comfort of our desks, home offices or workplaces in a given day now, if we are ever going to really make a difference in our lives and the lives of those we care for and love, we are in serious need of balance.

Reconnecting with the other passengers travelling with us on this journey we call life has never been easier as a simple "Hi", or "Good Morning", or even a "You look very nice today". The reason it may seem more difficult now is that we have been trained to feel more comfortable in an environment where anonymous one-way communication is the norm. Thinking about the possibility of two way communication where another person can respond "unpredictably" to our comments or intention of starting a conversation scares the hell out of us. We were isolated by these forces, so that these influencers can have sole ownership of our attention to exert their will and their messaging onto us in the most Orwellian of fashions, and now this has become comfortable for us.

I encourage everyone reading this book to reflect on your daily interactions and inputs, stand outside of yourself and witness the constant flow of messages being thrown at you and see how much of your time is being stolen by the constant competition for your attention. Once you are able to observe first-hand the vast amount time available to you within this pool of messaging and media, I would encourage each and every person to consciously make the decision to re-balance their time and attention. Making the decision and enabling that decision of course will take time, and you must safeguard that decision so you do not fall into the same trap over and over again, but decide now to make a change.

The buzzword when it comes to balance over the last decade has been "work-life balance". This is a great start but this should be defined a bit more to include YOU. Work is an obligation or commitment that most people do in order to fund their lives. Life is an all-encompassing measure of your existence outside of your workplace. The YOU in this equation sort of gets lost along the way and needs to be found if you plan to make any choices in your life at all, and it is through our relationships with those around us that help us discover who we really are. So as a final thought on this topic, I would encourage everyone to deliberately structure time in their schedules to: unplug themselves from anything that distracts from the real physical world around them; reconnect with family and friends by voice or face to face to catch up; practice connecting with new people on a social level; and make time to reconnect with themselves.

Unplug

Pop-ups, Dings, Spam, and Notifications – We are constantly bombarded by windows that jump onto our screen, sounds that alert us to emails or events, emails that carry messaging that we are not interested in, vibrating phones, and other notifications throughout our day. Some of these are set as a default when applications are installed or items are purchased, others we set in order to remind us of something important, and others come unexpectedly from unscrupulous sources trying to dupe us in some way. In all of these instances, however, these are distractions that shorten our attention span, heighten our anxiety, and negatively impact whatever we are doing. Even turning them off or unsubscribing from them is designed to be a challenge. In any case, part of the unplugging process is turning off all of these types of distractions, it may take some time to cover them all and you may miss a few here or there, but recapturing the time and focus available to you, and the lowering of your anxiety levels, will help deliver exponential gains in personal happiness and productivity in whatever you are doing. If you feel comfortable with this exercise, you can take it one step further by trying to avoid every kind of messaging you can think of for a short period of time, such as marketing, advertising, commercials, or any media that serves to insert a message into your brain. Just by thinking about how to do this should identify influencers such as television, radio, the internet, walking down an urban street, driving in urban areas or riding on transit. Each of these influencers deliver media in the form of ads, pop-ups, commercials, and other attention grabbers which I like to call **time killers**. Avoiding them will really help you unplug from outside influences, but it will be a challenge.

Unplug Worksheet

Exercise

Unplug – even for a short time – and document your experience. Choose as many influencers or distractions as you feel comfortable with and restructure your life for a set period of time to avoid their effect. You may want to start with a few hours in the evening, or on a weekend day, but do what you can to shut out the time killer. Do your best if you feel up to the task and make sure you document in your worksheet the effort you had to go through to complete this challenge. And don't be surprised if your anxiety level is heightened the first few times you consciously try to block out your time killers. Remember that you have been subconsciously trained to expect the constant bombardment of information, messaging, and media. Silencing it even for a few hours may seem unbearable at first, but it is the first step in recapturing this time for you to focus on and develop your own thoughts, ideas, goals, and dreams.

Rediscover

With the constant encroachment of our work into our lives and the addition of all the time killers eating away our focus and our sanity, it is hard enough getting in a few thoughts of your own on any given day. So when you do create the time based on completion of some of the exercises we worked through together, make a point to use a portion of that time to rediscover yourself, your life and the people you are travelling with on this planet we call Earth. With all the distractions in our daily lives, we sometimes forget that life just keeps rolling along whether we focus on it or not, and at a time that we do stop to take a look around, the landscape has entirely changed.

<u>Rediscover Worksheet</u>

Exercise

Sometimes it is easy for friends to pick-up right where they left off and other times it may be more difficult, but the important thing to notice in this exercise is the effect that the passage of time has on the resilience of friendships. Sometimes we forget that we are naturally social creatures and offering a spritely hello to a stranger and the potential for unmitigated chit-chat may lead you to actually have a more colorful and interesting day. Take a step to rediscover your natural inclination of being unreservedly social.

Decide to connect with someone, either a person you have not spoken to in a long time or even a complete stranger – document the experience, how did it go down, where were you, how did you approach the situation, how did it make you feel before, during and after the experience, and what was memorable about it.

Reconnect

Even though you may occupy the same space as someone else, or interact daily through routine and convenience, connecting with a person is a conscious activity that requires focused attention.

It is often our closest friends and loved ones that end up being alienated in the process of living our lives, but at this stage you should look to reconnect with them on a level that may be reminiscent of simpler times. You have made the time already. Now shift your focus on the most important people in your life and begin sharing some of your time and energy on them.

Reconnect Worksheet

Exercise

Make a short list of the important people in your life, friends, loved ones, etc. and schedule time over the next week to systematically touch base with each person by voice or in person to catch up with what is going on in their lives and share what is going on in yours. Reconnect and jot down some quick details in the worksheet provided about the experience.

Mindfulness

You've rediscovered friends and family you have not reached out to in a long time and you have consciously reconnected with your close family and loved ones to reconnect on a deeper level. Now it is time to reconnect with yourself. We often forget that we are people too and that silent reflection, having a coffee by ourselves, or participating in life's basic pleasures is something we need to enjoy once and a while as well. Being mindful about your own thoughts and wellbeing is a luxury in today's fast paced world, but the benefits are abundant, so take special note to perform this exercise with the intention of reintroducing yourself to yourself.

Mindfulness Worksheet

Exercise

Make time for yourself over the next week to use what you learned about unplugging from the world, and do something for you and you alone, with no distractions, totally focused on the task at hand. The task you choose could be anything you want and should take a minimum of 2 hours to complete, and a maximum of whatever time you feel you are comfortable with remaining unplugged. But like I said, no distractions from the outside world. No cellular phones, TV, media conferring devices, or time killers whatsoever.

Making Friends

Making friends may be easy or difficult for you, but the importance of growing your personal and professional network to achievement in many areas of your personal life and life change goals makes the effort worth it. We are all given the same amount of time each day in which to actualize what we want in our lives. When we look at influential people accomplishing extraordinary things, we often find a vast network of people supporting their effort to achieve their goals. Whether they are leaders in business, technology, scientific research, or faith, they seem able to accomplish more because of their support network. If you develop a network of support in any aspect of your life, you will also begin to achieve more in that area. Even if you feel uncomfortable with meeting new people, the value of a growing network can mean the difference between success and failure, happiness or unhappiness.

<u>Making Friends Template</u>

Exercise

Actively explore things happening in your life where people are getting together:

- Parties
- Group trips with a tour
- Night outs
- Church
- Work gatherings
- Events
- Community center programs
- Groups and clubs you can join
- Volunteering for charity work
- Etc.

List them all along with the frequency in which they meet. Choose one short term gathering, like a party or event, one medium term activity (max 8 weeks) like a course, and one long term activity like volunteer work, that will expand your network of friends and colleagues. Work them into your schedule and, starting with the short term activity through to the long term activity; engage in the social activities you have chosen from your list. Although meeting people face to face may seem out of fashion in the interconnected on-demand video-conferenced world in which we currently live, there is a deeper natural instinctual mechanism that delivers a wealth of social, behavioral, and biological benefits to person to person interaction.

Building your network not only enhances your life, it opens you up to other ways of thinking and provides access to opportunities that you may not have had.

Principled Living

Having opened your eyes a little to some of the not so common knowledge surrounding the lives we all lead on a daily basis in the areas of Financial, Personal, and Relationships, I want to introduce a simple concept to you that might alter the way you identify with the challenges I have identified so far through the exercises you have completed. So let's see if I can't open your mind to a few new ways to change the challenges you have identified into opportunities to transform them into areas of positive change. Once you have reviewed this section, feel free to go back and review some of the outcomes of the previous exercises in the areas of Financial, Personal Time and Relationships to reflect on how these strategies can be applied to make positive adjustments.

I am a firm believer in the concept of **Principled Living**. What this means is developing a set of rules or guiding principles for living your day to day life, and following those principles when certain events require guidance. The intentions of the principles are to lead you along a path to get to a particular place in your life. Having principles in place will make sure that you will not waiver from a path to something greater when obstacles are presented or your attention is drawn away. For example, if you have ever played the lottery, a little or even a lot, and come to the realization that you just are not a lucky person, you may set a principle in place that you will either never play the lottery again or at least limit your play to certain circumstances such as to purchase only one ticket and only during a draw with a very high jackpot value. Once you have committed to this principle and have it embedded into your mind, or on paper defined why you have set this as a principle, the next time you feel the urge to spend money on a random lottery or are enticed by the marketing for different types of lottery and gambling, you can reflect back on the principle you have created and follow the guidance you have laid out. Principled living is really a tool to strengthen your resolve and keep you focused on the things that are important in your life. Defining them involves being truthful to yourself, looking forward to a better future, and capturing the essence of what a path to that future would look like. Defining your principles and following them will preserve your forward momentum to achieve your goal.

Now I know what you may be thinking … well, I don't want my life to be predefined by a set of rules, because I am a free spirit and should be able to live my life the way I want. Or, I am already confined by rules wherever I go, in the laws that govern, the rules at my job, and all the rules that confine my life on a day to day basis already, I don't need any more rules!

I totally get where you are coming from, but you need to realize one simple fact … you are already applying the concept of Principled Living in your life right now. Everyone has rules and limits that they place on themselves on a subconscious level. You may come to realize this through a gut feeling in your stomach when faced with a decision or event, through a conscious decision made when a friend has dared you to do something, or through the little voice inside your head that guides you in a morally challenging decision in your life. These gut checks, little voices, and whatever else you want to call these manifestations, are a result of your mind and body reacting to the principles you subconsciously have imposed on your own life. The idea of principled living is to use the mechanism you are already applying daily, toward consciously guiding your life in a particular direction. Instead of letting your subconscious mind decide what it thinks is best for your sense of morality, manifesting your innermost fears, and digging up your childhood to allow your past life to infinitely impact your future, you have the ability to consciously change this system to work FOR you, starting today.

The first step in having Principled Living work FOR you is to identify what your goals are, what you want to work toward, and the overall direction you want your life to take. Most people are use to following a routine in their daily life and instead of entirely eliminating the notion of a routine causing them to feel lost without it, principled living is a way to use what we currently have that works in our lives. Principled living slowly transforms the idea of routine and repetition from a negative aspect of our lives (i.e. a rut), into a positive aspect of our lives that will constantly enhance and build our lives in the direction we want it to go. Principled living is the creation of rules to live by, which provide **in the moment guidance** at key decision making points in our daily lives. Your principles are created out of deep thought and reflection, and enabled in a ceremonial and powerful event to signify a change in direction. Some people may have only a couple of rules to live by and others may want their lives to be governed to a great extent by a plethora of predetermined rules to ensure their path to a prosperous future is clearly identified and defined. Also, these defining principles should be reviewed at set intervals to ensure they are current and remain valid. I usually recommend in my Principled Living Workshops that participants review their personal principles at least twice a year. Using principled living in your daily life is leveraging your own mind's mechanism to automate your actions or reactions to certain events or decisions. By implanting a set of guiding principles to govern or predetermine an action, you are safeguarding the direction that you are choosing or the path that you are on, when decision points present themselves to try and derail you from your goals. To a certain extent, it is automating your journey to the successful achievement of your goal. Like your custom auto-pilot to achieving success.

At this point, reflect back on what you have learned through the exercises you have completed about your Financial Life, your Personal Life, and your Relationships, as I have walked you through in the last few sections of this book. Now envision the direction of your life prior to completing any of the exercises, as if it were to continue in that direction in perpetuity, for the remainder of your life. This would be the current direction of your life in these specific areas. Now if you are happy the way things currently stand in each of those areas, then you are already enlightened enough to have foreseen your path and are living your dream life. If you are like the remaining 99.999999% of the world, then let's get to work and start building your dream life together.

<u>Principled Living Worksheet</u>

Exercise

Starting from your current state in the areas described, you will identify what you would like that area of your life to look like in its ideal sense, as defined in your mind. So for example, in the area of relationships, you could describe your ideal life as being happily married, with two children, a specific number of friends and how often you would typically interact with them. The quality of the relationships, such as a small group of 20-30 close friends that you would connect with regularly, travel with , and share your deepest thoughts with. The next 20-30 could be defined as emerging close friends that are up-and-coming to the close friends category, wherein you connect a bit less frequently and where although you have never travelled with them or attended their children's birthday parties, you would like to explore those options one day to see how the relationship evolves. And, the remaining friends could be acquaintances that you are cordial to but limit interactions to the gym, the playground when your kids are playing, neighborly conversation, and the like. Define elements in each category in as much detail as you can, in their ideal sense.

So start with a couple of key areas of your life, take some time to create these definitions on where you are now and what the ideal state for these areas would be. At the completion of your definition process, review your list from top to bottom to make sure it accurately describes what you are looking for in a starting place and in a destination. After you have done this, isolate each specific area and define in writing, specific events, situations, and decisions that occur fairly frequently that can be seen as path markers that have the opportunity to change the direction of your path. With the example above, it could be invitations to an event, or a request to have dinner. A situation could be someone opening up to you about a personal problem. After you identify these path markers, group any similar items together. Finally, review the groups and develop a simple statement that captures the definition of the group and that provides an action statement that is consistent with the direction you would like your path to evolve toward in the future. For example, if your future goal would be to have more close friends, you may write a statement that indicates in any situation where you meet a new person or connect with an existing friend, you consciously try to introduce the idea of a social meeting in the future, such as a dinner invitation, coffee, invitation to a gathering of some sort, or whatever would take the relationship from where it is right now to a closer friendship. This blanket rule would provide you with guidance whenever you are put into a situation where you can further a relationship in the direction of your desired outcome.

Continue working through the other areas you have identified and come up with at least 6-8 general rules like the one in the example that would provide a clear direction to you that is consistent with a specific area goal. For financial goals, it could be as simple as emptying your pocket of change into a jar at the end of each day and making a deposit into a special savings account monthly to create a small emergency fund or nest egg. For your emotional well-being, it could be to select at least 2-3 of your closest friends and to open up about new challenges in your life that you have not already discussed, to provide you with an emotional safe zone. Whatever areas you would like to define in this exercise, begin to gain an awareness of the subconscious mechanism operating in the background, and do your best to consciously interject your goals and your path through development of your guiding principles.

Once complete, you will have in your hand the beginning of a set of guiding principles that you will apply daily to deliver you to your ideal life. As you progress through the remainder of this book, I will offer other thoughts about areas to include in your principled living model. At the completion of this book, you should revisit the information you have written and slowly begin editing, adding or subtracting items from your list until you are happy that it embodies all the areas in your life that you are not currently happy with, and provides simple and broad direction for you in times of reflection and decision. Incorporate your principled living strategy into your life immediately so that you can start benefiting from its powerful influence, and revisit your list at least once a year to make sure it continues to deliver results and that it remains relevant to your goals.

Health – Your Physical Wellbeing

Many people have varying opinions on the ideal physical wellbeing of individuals of all walks of life. But there are a few key observations that we can all make about our current state of health and the environments in which we have to manage our health.

Food

Other people control our food and what it is comprised of. From fluorine in our drinking water to genetically modified crops, additives and preservatives, coloring agents and artificial sweeteners, hormones and pesticides, the planetary food supply chain has changed in unimaginable ways over the last few decades. It is now left in the hands of legislators, administrators and scientists to decide what is good or bad for us to eat, and there is mounting evidence to show that they have not been acting in OUR best interests. Who does have influence and the power to change the direction of the food industry? Large lobbying agencies, special interest groups, the largest corporate food producers in the world, essentially the people with the deepest pockets. Think of this like a Salary plus Bonus employment arrangement from the perspective of the people making decisions about our food supply and ultimately your health. The salary component is covered by your tax dollars, but our taxes are taken regardless of what happens so their base salary remains fairly consistent. The bonus part is when all of these parties that have vested interests in government policies surrounding the growing, manufacturing, production and distribution of food get together and throw lots of money at the people that are supposed to be acting on our best interests, to shift their focus to support the industry or corporate interest. We hear about it almost every day in the media, with stories of new allergies, new health risks, and the adverse effects that our enhanced food products are producing on a broad scale.

Physical Exercise

Statistics have consistently identified a growing epidemic of obesity around the world over the last two decades. Food however is only part of this equation. Lifestyle and activity levels play the other main role in the weight equation. In the developed world, we have seen our work lives grow to fully consume our daily existence, with long hours, sedentary work environments, the expectation of constant availability, and the pressure placed on individuals by their employers to produce more and more. If there were 40 hours in a day, the work would expand to fill the additional time too. So in this environment, how many people can regularly visit the gym, or use the expensive home gym equipment they bought several years ago? The thick layer of dust on the home equipment and the unused gym memberships clearly tell the tale. We don't have time seems to be the consensus.

Escape

The high stress of our daily lives now drives us to drink, literally. Global alcohol consumption rates have been rising over the last 3 decades. In addition to this, we are now collectively smoking more, doing more drugs (prescription, over the counter, and illegal), getting high and looking for more and different ways to escape from our everyday reality with as little effort as possible. This downward spiral is leading us toward a medical, physiological, and psychological disaster. Now there are pills for just about everything you can imagine. We have become a pill popping generation, and we get the push from both sides. The health industry is pushing vitamin pills, herbal pills, supplements, Chinese medicine, Ayurvedic concoctions, Naturopathic and Holistic drops, pills, and cleansing formulas. The inside of your local health food store now looks a lot like the inside of a drug store. And on the flip side, the pharmaceutical industry is constantly bombarding us with the newest and greatest pills to do anything from manage childhood depression, combat pain in every orifice and appendage, and give men that well-earned erection. The medical, psychological and psychiatric professions are producing new labels for new conditions or disorders with rapid frequency, from ADHD to Oppositional Defiant

Disorder, from Caffeine-Induced Sleep Disorder to Wendigo Psychosis, from Alice in Wonderland Syndrome to Foreign Accent Syndrome. The labelling of a condition or disorder leads to the development of a treatment plan for it, which means the doctor can associate the condition or disorder to the pills needed to treat or manage it. This is a nice and neat method of treating the complexity of human ailments. And in some instances, during the testing and development of new drugs, some unforeseen side-effects have been discovered that have been developed into the treatment of unintended disorders. Imagine that! A mistake turns into a commercially viable drug to treat a disorder that it was not intended to treat. Wow, the medical industry IS creative, isn't it? Magic Beans or Magic Pills … is there a difference?

Ideal Health

Our physical and emotional wellbeing is our burden to bear and ours alone. Because we live in our bodies and nourish it on a daily basis, we manage all of the inputs that derive the outcome of our own health. Our choices of food, drink, and activity have the direct and only inputs to our health. Now our inaction also has an impact on our health too, so not being active, not drinking water, and not reading labels also has an impact on our health. Ignorance is no excuse. Now at this point in time, there are a ton of influences from all directions pushing every imaginable agenda with relation to health, that prey on unwitting people with their endless array of lies. There is the "love your body whatever shape it is" group, the "get lean and mean" group, the "take pills to lose weight" group, and even the organic living group that has built its own industry around organic choices. Whether you are fat or thin, old or young, wrinkled or hairy, YOU are in full control of your health situation and you are always able to make changes to meet a specific goal. Not only that, you can do this without spending any more money, you can do this without counting calories, and you can do this without strenuous sweat sessions at the gym three days a week for 45 minutes a session.

Eyes Wide Open

The first step in exploring YOUR ideal health is to help open your eyes to the world around you by tweaking your routine ever so slightly. I will show you how taking a macro-health approach will deliver gains that you never thought possible with simple flexible rules that will help you focus on and remember you goals, and virtually automate their achievement. Again, YOU will be in control of the rules you set and will be able to adjust them along the way to suit the lifestyle you want to achieve.

The three key areas in developing a healthier physical you are: food; exercise; and, mental wellbeing. Food nourishes your body and provides the vital energy to think and do all those enjoyable things in your life that are worth pursuing. Exercise keeps your body moving well, helps fight old age, promotes your body's natural ability to fight disease, and delivers mental happiness through physical means. Lastly, mental wellbeing helps you maintain focus on all of your goals and directly impacts the results of all other efforts to manage your health, either positively or negatively. If you're eating habits and exercise routine remain consistent yet you are experiencing fluctuations in your ability to focus, losing sleep, gaining or losing weight, you are most likely in need of a mental wellbeing checkup.

So let us work through a few exercises to open your eyes and then revisit this conversation as the results come in.

Before we start, let's just gather a bit of information now to use as a point of reference after we work through the exercises.

Health Now – Daily Worksheet

Print 7 Copies

Health Now

The Health Now worksheet is designed to help you easily capture vital health information on a daily basis for a period of one week. This information will become your personal baseline to compare against the impact of any changes that you make to achieve health related goals. Capturing your daily routine will include gathering information about the following:

- Wake and sleep times
- General overall feeling on waking, at lunch, and at bed time
- Start weight
- Times when major meals and snacks are eaten: Breakfast, Lunch, Dinner and snacks
- Where food is eaten: Home, Restaurant, Takeaway, Office lunch, etc.
- Eating alone or with others: Alone at home, Out with friend, Business lunch with co-workers, etc.
- For snacks, break down by number of sweet versus salty snacks
- Number of healthy meals versus unhealthy meals per day, week
- Number of glasses of water consumed in a day
- Number of cans or bottles of pop, cups of coffee or tea a day
- Amount of alcohol consumed per day, week
- Number of cigarettes, cigars, or pipe smokes per day

- Other drugs consumed per day, week including marijuana, illicit drugs, etc.
- Number of hours of TV watched in a day
- Number of hours worked per day, week (both at work or outside of work, i.e. checking emails, thinking about work related items, etc.
- Time spent deliberately exercising per day, week (type of exercise)

Over the course of one 7 day week, complete one worksheet per day.

Health Now – Consolidated Worksheet

At the completion of this one week baseline period, collect all daily worksheets and assemble the information into the consolidate worksheet. Once this step is complete, we can now begin demonstrating the power of principled living as it applies to your health and make some suggestions that will have a positive impact on your health.

Exercise 1 - Food

Using the information from the Food and Drink section of your consolidated worksheet, identify the following information:

- Average Wake time
- Average Sleep time
- Times that breakfast, lunch and dinners are eaten

I will now list some simple rules for you to incorporate into your daily life for a period of one week and then you will reference the numbers to see what has changed.

Our Food – Grocery Shopping Checklist

This exercise will begin with a trip to the supermarket and a permanent marker. Let's begin with a brief primer about supermarket layout. Typically a supermarket is laid out to have basic fresh and frozen foods on the outside walls of the building and foods that are processed in the center aisles. Without knowing how much you spend on groceries per week or what specifically you purchase, we will design rules that can be easily applied to everyone's shopping lists and to keep you in control of the choices of products. So here is what you will need to do to prepare for your exercise:

- The preference is to begin this process on a weekend day. Either day will do.
- With your total budget value for this shopping trip, separate 80% and 20% of the dollar value.
- With the 80% you will only by items from the fresh areas of your supermarket, excluding the bakery. This will include fresh fruits, vegetables, meats, cheeses, fish, and dairy (excluding items with sugar added).
- The remaining 20% can be spent on anything else in the store, but should include at least 2 cases of six 1.5 liter bottles of water
- When you arrive home and unpack your groceries, you will mark each item with a symbol or your initials so that they can be easily identified and then pack them away in their normal place in your kitchen. Let any other family members or others with access to the kitchen know that they should not use anything marked with your special symbol or initials.
- For the bottles of water, minimum of 12 total, you will mark them with the numbers 1 and two so that you have 6 sets of 2 water bottles.

Our Food – Weekly Challenge

And here is my set of pilot rules for you to stick to for one week, using only the items you purchased on your shopping list. Print off this list and take it with you so that you can reference the rules throughout the day and check them off as you achieve each rule within the day. Here we go:

- Within 30 minutes of waking, drink 1-2 glasses of water.
- Within 1 hour of waking, eat breakfast. Breakfast must include protein in any form you like.
- Avoid adding salt to any meals or snacks.
- Only drink caffeinated drinks in your home or at your workplace. Pick one place only.
- When leaving your home for work, take one set (marked 1 and 2) of water bottles.
- Between the time you leave your home and the time you go to bed, you will do your best to drink the water in both 1.5 liter bottles of water (3 liters in total).
- Any snacks you eat must be from the items you bought at the supermarket i.e. no outside snacks.

- Lunch can be anything you want from the items bought at the supermarket or from any outside source like a restaurant, café, office lunch, etc. but must be at least half comprised of vegetables grown above ground i.e. not potatoes or root vegetables.
- Dinner should be the last thing eaten in your day and should contain less than ¼ of protein. It can be eaten from items purchased at the supermarket or can be outside food, just be aware if ordering in a restaurant, to let the server know the proportions of protein to other items on the plate so that they can help guide your choice to meet those proportions.
- No alcohol or caffeinated beverages should be consumed after eating dinner.
- Dinner should be eaten at least 2 hours before going to sleep.
- Just before bed, drink at least one glass of water.
- Feel free to take notes throughout the week of any positive or negative things you notice.

That's it!!

You will notice that this list is not a detailed breakdown of what you should eat, when you should eat it, and in what quantity you should consume. There is a lot of choice and the choices remain with you for what you are buying at the supermarket, what you are selecting when you are eating at a restaurant, available snacks, and when you choose to eat. Setting up a simple routine like this will help you think about what you are eating and can help you think broadly about easy choices and rules that can be decided and tweaked for your lifestyle, and that will have the biggest impact to your day to day health.

Our Food – Weekly Challenge - Results

Follow this routine for a week and then answer the following questions:

- Has your weight changed
- Did you ever feel starved of food
- How do you feel generally
- List any positive or negative changes you have noticed
- What would you change in this routine to better suit your specific needs, to enhance the positive changes you noted and reduce the negative changes you listed
- Is this routine list or your adjusted list sustainable over a long period

This exercise is a great way to start you thinking about simple ways to make consistent changes to your daily routine for the largest impact. If you feel up to another round, complete the same exercise but incorporating your revised list of rules. At the same time, we will work through the next exercise for physical health so that you can do them both in unison. Let's see if we can't kick start your path to ideal health together.

Physical Exercise Worksheet

Exercise 2 - Physical Exercise

For this exercise, you will need to following information from your initial data sheet:

- Start weight
- Time spent deliberately exercising per day, week (type of exercise)
- General overall feeling on waking, at lunch and at bed time.

Using the same methodology of principled living, I will outline some basic rules to be incorporated into your daily routine for the next 7 days. Keep in mind that everyone is at different levels of fitness and if you feel uncomfortable at any point or unable to complete an exercise due to physical ailment, disability or injury that is totally ok. Just move on to the next item on the list. Notice I have not asked you at all about any weight loss goals or specific performance targets you may wish to achieve. We'll revisit this at the end of this exercise. Here are the rules of this exercise:

- On waking and before bed, do any stretches you wish to at least 4 different body parts.
- At least 3 days during the week, travel with a friend at least 15 minute by foot to eat your lunch. This could mean walking 15 minutes to a restaurant or café, or 15 minutes to a local park to enjoy your meal outside. In whatever form you choose, just make sure it is at least 15 minutes each way. Have fun with this by choosing an out of the way lunch destination and bringing a buddy with you.
- At least 4 days a week, go out for a leisurely stroll right after dinner for at least 30 minutes, preferably with a friend or loved one, but if it's just you and your music, that's ok too.
- Whenever you see an escalator, treat it like the plague and take the stairs. (Now this one is only if you feel up to it. Not everyone has the same level of mobility, and if you are at all uncomfortable with doing this, by all means avoid it.)
- If you have a regular exercise routine, continue to follow your routine.
- Feel free to take notes throughout the week of any positive or negative things you notice.

That's it for this exercise. A basic, simple routine that is easy to incorporate into your week. Again you can print off this short list and put a checkmark beside each items as you complete it.

Physical Exercise - Results

Once you have completed the week, let's revisit the list from the data sheet.

- Has your weight changed, if so how much
- How do you feel generally
- List any positive or negative changes you have noticed
- What would you change in this routine to better suit your specific needs, to enhance the positive changes you noted and reduce the negative changes you listed
- Is this routine list or your adjusted list sustainable over a long period

Again, you are looking to enable simple ways to make consistent changes to your daily routine for the largest impact. This process is about doing your best to build a simple routine into your life that will set you on the right path and build your capability to do more later. Now for anyone that already has a specific goal in mind for losing weight, gaining weight, transforming their body in some way, or achieving a specific performance target, let's work on incorporating those goals into your routine. Again using the idea of principled living, set your mind toward where you are now and where you are looking to be in your ideal state. Define what you are looking to do with a statement and an action. Now in the process of developing a working set of principles, you want to look at your specific history of physical, mental and emotional challenges and honestly detail the specifics of those challenges. For example, if you have always had a weakness for chocolate, then document that in your historical record. Or if you have had an injury that prevents you from specific types of exercise, then add this information as well. Once your notes are completed, review your list and develop some simple principles that will guide you in the right direction with respect to your goals. If you are happy with your list, enable it for at least a month but track your progress once a week to make sure you are heading in the right direction. You should also feel comfortable talking to your close friends and family about what you are doing, so that they can lend any support they can throughout the process. Remember, you are never truly alone and can always find someone to talk to. After the month is over, revisit your goal and see the progress you have made toward achieving it. Also review your rules to see if any need tweaking in order to achieve your goal, and make any adjustments you feel are needed. Once you are happy with your progress and your list, continue doing what you have been doing until your goal has been met.

So far, you have gone through two exercises. Not sure if you've noticed but neither exercise is highly visible, maximum effort, counting this and that, with lots of busy work and whatnot. Wow, I think I burned 100 calories just writing that phrase. The point is this; slow and steady wins the race and especially with weight changes and your health, long term consistent application of positive changes will guarantee positive results. The more you can accomplish without thinking too much about the process, the more results you will see over time. Focus more on creating personal principles you are comfortable with, looking at the results of those principles in action, and adjusting the principles to maximize the positive results. For those readers who feel excited about having completed the second round of the Ideal Health Triple Crown, and want to shoot for the gold, try one more round of exercise one and two, while incorporating Exercise 3 into the mix.

Methods of Escape Worksheet

Exercise 3 - Methods of Escape

This exercise is all about personal vices in your life. We know they have an impact on our health and we know that there is a cost financially, emotionally, and spiritually. Vices come in many forms and can be characterized in many ways, but we will just take a simple approach to focus on reducing their impact for a short amount of time to see what the effects are to your wellbeing.

Using the information from the initial data sheet, you will need the following information:

- Number of sweet versus salty snacks consumed in a day, week
- Number of cans or bottles of pop, cups of coffee or tea a day
- Amount of alcohol consumed per day, week
- Number of cigarettes, cigars, pipe per day
- Number of hours of TV watched in a day
- Number of hours worked per day, week (both at work or outside of work, i.e. checking emails, thinking about work related items, etc.)

Over the next 7 days, incorporate these basic rules into your daily routine. Here are the rules of this exercise:

- Follow the first two exercises while completing this exercise.
- Pick two days in the week that will be your cheat days.
- On the selected cheat days only, you can eat or drink any of the salty or sweet snacks, caffeinated drinks or alcohol, but only at the times indicated in exercise one.

- For smokers, set aside exactly half of what you would normally consume in a week into a separate container, be it a plastic sandwich bag, cigar or cigarette case of another suitable container. Feel free to smoke at any times you wish, but just budget your consumption to not exceed what you have set aside. You may want to also pack some gum along with your smoking products to give you a choice come the time.
- For users of illicit drugs, commit at least 2 hours during the week exploring the impact of drug use on your health and looking into available cessation programs or support groups in your area.
- On days other than your cheat days, on leaving your workplace, you will turn off your work related mobile device, leave your computer at your workplace and commit to not checking your emails or even thinking about work once you leave.
- Also, on days other than your cheat days, you will spend at least an hour of time on each day, which would have been spent watching television, reaching out and connecting by voice or face to face with a friend or loved one. Electronic communication and social media are not an option.
- Feel free to take notes throughout the week of any positive or negative things you notice.

Methods of Escape - Results

At the end of the week, review your initial data and let's see what has changed by answering these questions:

- How do you feel generally
- List any positive or negative changes you have noticed
- Have the changes you have made this week impacted any of the results from the other two exercises
- Did you save any money by reducing your consumption and if so, how much
- What was the reaction from the people you connected with by voice or face to face
- What would you change in this routine to better suit your specific needs, to enhance the positive changes you noted and reduce the negative changes you listed
- Is this routine list or your adjusted list sustainable over a long period

Although addiction is a frequently used word for consumers of alcohol and tobacco, social support for their use is a partial contributing factor of continuing use. Many programs would promote cutting alcohol and tobacco use altogether as an extreme method to remove temptation. What is more important here is that you begin to notice the difference between having it in your life and having less of it in your life. You are your own judge and only you can recognize the value of eliminating a vice from your life. This exercise is about showing you that you have a choice and what that choice looks like so that you can make an informed decision about the path you want to take moving forward. Many successful programs are available for free to help you combat many forms of addiction so if you have reached a time in your life where you feel it is right to explore your options, reach out to local support groups, a medical doctor, or trusted friends to find a program that meets your needs.

Automating your Health

Most of us have a daily routine that we follow. Our routines have developed over much of our lives and they have become so comfortable over time that we may not even realize they are there. This is a great benefit when it comes to overall health and physical wellbeing as we are creatures of habit, and replacing an unhealthy habit with a healthy one is really easy to do. And with your health, it is the small changes that tend to make the largest impact. In the exercises later on in this book, we will walk you through what you can do immediately to start changing your focus to a healthier future. But like I said earlier, and every step of the way, the choice is always yours. If you are happy with the way you are, then nobody including I should be telling you what is good for you. If you would like to make a change and need some ideas or a place to start, then I am here to help support you to the level you want. This is a totally custom solution for your life where YOU choose the items you want from my buffet of suggestions and advice.

Ideal Health – CONCLUSIONS

<u>Ideal Health – Conclusions Form</u>

Compile your results from the three brief exercises and review the results you have noted at the end of each exercise to determine the following:

- What has changed both positively and negatively during the exercises
- Looking at the positive and negative changes in the three key areas, which factors contributed to the positive changes and which factors contributed to the negative changes in each exercise
- List 3-5 ways you can promote or enhance each of the positive changes listed in your exercises and list 3-5 ways you can reduce or eliminate the negative changes listed in your exercises

- Using your lists of enhancing the positive and reducing the negative changes exercise, develop a simple framework of rules that you can apply on a daily basis that would capture the essence of your lists as it would broadly apply to your life
- What have you learned about yourself during this exercise

Developing simple to follow and reference rules to account for your daily health and wellbeing that you can easily remember under a variety of different circumstances is the simplest way to automate good health and healthy living. This approach is consistent with our discussion above about principled living and following these exercises as a guide and modifying them to enhance your day to day life will lead you on a path to your ideal health. Make sure to take the time to revisit these exercises at least a few times a year to set new goals and adjust your personalized rules to better capture changes in your life.

The Human Struggle

Nobody is immune to struggle. Be us rich or poor, white or of color, educated or not, we all have our own very personal and specific struggles to resolve. Rich or poor could both abuse the same substances. White or colored can both become depressed. Educated or uneducated are both susceptible to weight issues. Everyone is capable of losing faith. We all struggle in our own way and in our own time. It is part of being human and these moments of struggle are opportunities for us to take a moment of pause and reflect on our lives and our positions, so that we can change course and make things better. Struggle is part of the human condition and should always be seen as a temporary event in our lives. In our minds however, there is a mechanism that prompts us to think about why a negative event has happened to us and this mechanism can consume our emotional, psychological, and physiological wellbeing paralyzing us to act in any way. It is during moments like this that our will is tested and that we must fight inertia from setting in. It at this time that we must renew our focus, determination and resilience to achieve the goals we set for ourselves and reach for our dreams with the faith that we have the tools to succeed. In the exercises you have completed, a deliberate addition to each stage was an emotional check, because it is vitally important for all of us to actively gage the mental and emotional impact of our actions. Being fully present is your own life allows you to witness the state and effect of events on your own life as an active participant instead of a passenger. Building this awareness will help you refine your personal principles to mental, emotional, and spiritual wellbeing. This process is an organic one that stems from all that you do and all that you are, so build a consciousness of your world and create the principles you need to bind all other aspects of your life with a consistent and pervasive positive wellbeing.

If you have reached for this book in a time of need in search of guidance, it is my sincere hope that even a small aspect of this book can resonate with you and better your life.

The World does not Stop for You

Although we would all like to think that we are the center of our own universe, the reality that the world keeps on going with or without our involvement is evident. Whether we participate or not, the world stops for no one. If you would like to test this fact, reserve a day in which you do nothing at all aside from the basic functions of relaxing, eating, and performing simple activities on your own. No TV, no cellular phone, no contact with anyone aside from direct family. Then at the end of the day, turn on the news, check your Facebook or twitter accounts, check your phone messages, and see how much you have missed. And this is just in a single day. We have so many interactions with people and are constantly bombarded with information on a daily basis keeping us abreast of what is happening all around the globe that turning it off and creating a day's backlog is almost unthinkable. The fact that we can feel quite anxious when we are cut off from the world like this is another example of how we have become slaves to the brainwashing effects of this endless minutia. In fact, we are swept away every day in a whirlwind of routine, occupation, events, media, entertainment, information, and other diversions that most of us never even think to stop and take a look at what is going on or what has changed. A simple way to envision this effect is to ask yourself, if things remained the same in your life as they are now, what would things look like in 5 years, 10 years, or 20 years? The same career path, the same relationships, the same daily routine, the same life. Projecting your life forward to the future tends to give you a perspective on where things are now and if there are things you are not happy about your life now, think about how unhappy you will be given the passing of another 5 or 10 years. Each passing year will be another lost opportunity to change your life, follow through on your resolutions, and continue on a path of bitterness and regret. Yes, the world will keep on rolling ahead with or without us, but it is the realization that we must all come to that we have a choice and can redesign our interactions with the world as we know it, and structure this system in a way to keep you focused on only what you feel is important and valuable.

Doing the Same Thing Will Ensure You Fall Behind

As the world keeps moving forward, the expectation is that we follow along. Learning new things to stay current basically means that you have to continuously upgrade your knowledge and understanding to stay right where you are. If we look back at life a mere 50 years ago and reflect on how far we have come since then, the vast amounts of additional work we are now capable of in a day versus what was possible before, the amount of information available at our fingertips, and our ability to collaborate and communicate in real time without geographic boarders, our progress is truly staggering. Now imagine if at this time you said to yourself, that's it. I am no longer going to learn anything new. I will only continue doing what I am doing for the remainder of my days. What would happen? The world will keep going, keep producing new technologies, revealing new knowledge, and expecting more from us in order to stay exactly where we are. We are expected to keep doing more, learning more, and creating more so that we can stay exactly where we are. And if we merely continue to do the same thing that we have been doing, we fall behind. This is what we have been told by those that have authority over us as a method of controlling our day, keeping us occupied, and keeping us working. We are so busy keeping up with these expectations that at the end of each day, we are exhausted at even the thought of doing "more" to better our situations and our lives. Again, you have been duped into thinking that someone else owns your life and all your time. Don't let yourself be lied to!

I will tell you again plainly and simply, "YOU" are in control of your life, your time, and your future. The choice has always been available to you but many of us have difficulty getting past the idea of the consequences of taking action to break free. You can redesign your life on your own terms and achieve anything you want but you have to shift your focus away from learning for someone else and begin learning for yourself. Learning to create systems and projects, structure goals and interact with new people, reconnect with the world around you and with yourself to discover the eternal and unchanging knowledge that has transformed the world for thousands of years. The knowledge you will learn in the remainder of this book is all you will need for the rest of your life, and knowing, adapting, and applying this knowledge will free you from the constant pressure looking to control your life.

Make a Decision, ANY DECISION!
You have the power to change anything you want in your life

I have heard it many times by many people … making a decision is hard. They are dead wrong. Making a decision and choosing to do something different is easy. It is living with the consequences of decisions that is hard. So hard in fact that it paralyses most people from doing anything at all. More powerful than fear, this type of paralysis breaks down the will, dulls pain, creates stagnation, and leads people to a downward spiral that will suck happiness from all areas of life.

For whatever reason you are reading this book, make a promise to yourself that you make "YOUR" decision today.

Do it for you.

Do it for your family.

Do it for love and wellbeing.

Do it for financial security.

For whatever reason, choose a path and decide to follow it to wherever it leads.

Remember: A decision is not a death sentence. We are flexible, adaptable, ever changing, and can make course corrections along the way.

A lot of people, either consciously or subconsciously, believe change is inherently bad or leads to negative outcomes. There are two types of change: change that we initiate; and change that others initiate that have an impact on us.

Change initiated by us tends to be subjected to those same pesky consequences that paralyze us from action: fear of the unknown; fear that you are making a mistake or will make your current situation worse.

Change initiated by others tend to instill fear, and we are now thrust into a situation whereby we are forced to review all potential impacts of the change, causing people to lose sleep, look for an escape, and other negative behaviors detrimental to health and wellbeing.

Change is constant and for better or worse, we all need to develop strategies to deal with change in a positive way to ensure our interests are represented and our life is impacted in a way consistent with our goals.

What is Project Management?
In a Nutshell – A Less than 5 Minute Read

So if you haven't guessed already, I have been talking broadly in this first section about projects and project management. Now the word "project" is really overused by society today, so much so that it dilutes what it truly means. To make things worse, the title of Project Manager (**PM**) in workplaces around the world is often given out to people who are totally unskilled at managing projects successfully. The frequent assumption is that persons highly skilled in: software development, construction, engineering sciences, or numerous other professions; are properly equipped to manage a project related to their field of study. This assumption contributes to the fact that over 90% of projects fail to meet expectations or achieve their intended outcomes. Many companies and organizations do not know what a project manager does or how they can help, but they know that they need one. Projects completed with a capable and experienced project manager at the helm have a much higher percentage of success than those without. Furthermore, as companies and organizations become more mature at managing projects through the framework provided, use the techniques I will detail in this book, and develop experience with their staff participating in project teams managing smaller and then larger projects, over time they get better and better at it. This makes "Mature Projectized" companies and organizations much more capable of completing large complex projects successfully.

Why should this matter to you, you might ask? As corporations, governments, and other organizations get better and better at protecting and promoting their interests and designing projects to capture more market share, increase efficiency and profitability, and consolidate power, there is less of an opportunity for the individual to represent their interests and carve out their little piece of the happiness pie. And it is getting increasingly clear that these commercial interests are getting further and further away from addressing the needs of the global village. When trillions of dollars are spent around the globe on defense, space exploration, and scientific research in areas that will never directly impact the quality of life for the vast majority of the global population, while at the same time poverty, disease, access to clean water and appropriate sanitation, environmental destruction, and species endangerment are increasing at catastrophic levels to the point that our own very survival as a species may soon be at risk, you have to realize there is a problem. Other interests are drowning out the interests of the individual and of entire societies. And to a certain extent, knowledge of project management has contributed to this result.

You see, project management is knowledge available to everyone, for any purpose. It is about achieving goals … any goals. Should those goals be good or bad, constructive or destructive, project management provides a mechanism and processes to help work toward achieving them. And for the most part, corporations around the globe, governments and large organizations have used this knowledge to ensure their interests reign supreme. Now I am not saying that every corporation, government, or other body using project management is an evil empire of greed and destruction. In fact, over the many years I have spent consulting the largest most successful companies in the world, it is more often the case that these corporations want to build a better and more supportive relationship with their employees but simply need guidance to achieve this reality. What I am saying is that it is time for every individual to ensure their voice is heard, their interests are validated, and their dreams are fulfilled. This book is intended to level the playing field to keep large commercial and government interests in check and to protect the interests of every individual who chooses to raise their voice. Additionally, all of these parties benefitting from the application of project management within their enterprises should realize that promoting project management knowledge throughout their workforce for application both personally and professionally to achieve life and career goals are empowering their village with the tools to enhance their collective contribution. Happy and personally successful employees drive innovation and supply an endless stream of new ideas that can provide enduring benefit to all parties. Whether employers come to this realization or not, let us shift our focus back to you.

As we walk together through this process and work through the first areas in your life that you want to change, you will also get better at this process and over time you will be able to affect great change in your life and in the life of those around you. You will be able to tackle the most complex projects that you design and continue to apply more and more complex tools to help you achieve success in all areas of your life.

The Project Management Institute (PMI) defines a project like this:

"It's a temporary endeavor undertaken to create a unique product, service or result.

A project is temporary in that it has a defined beginning and end in time, and therefore defined scope and resources.

And a project is unique in that it is not a routine operation, but a specific set of operations designed to accomplish a singular goal. So a project team often includes people who don't usually work together – sometimes from different organizations and across multiple geographies.

The development of software for an improved business process, the construction of a building or bridge, the relief effort after a natural disaster, the expansion of sales into a new geographic market — all are projects." ("What is Project Management?", 2015 Project Management Institute, Inc., http://www.pmi.org/About-Us/About-Us-What-is-Project-Management.aspx)

PMI also defines project management like this:

"Project management, then, is the application of knowledge, skills, tools, and techniques to project activities to meet the project requirements." ("What is Project Management?", 2015 Project Management Institute, Inc., http://www.pmi.org/About-Us/About-Us-What-is-Project-Management.aspx)

Projects form the basis for much of the things you see around you in your daily life. They can be as small as designing a new menu at a local restaurant; to as large and complex as building the Large Hadron Collider which reveals clues to our physical universe. Going back thousands of years to the building of engineering wonders such as the Great Pyramids, Stonehenge and the Great Wall of China, right up until today in the design of electronic products, cars, roads, businesses, and the world that surrounds us, project management and projects have had a pervasive impact on our lives and of generations past. And it is project management and projects that drive the world forward with new technological and medical advancements, media and entertainment, consumer goods, and much of the complex world you encounter on a daily basis.

In as much as project management has been used for positive gains in human history, we must also understand that it is a tool and that any tool can be used in a constructive or destructive way. Projects that have expanded our knowledge of the universe have been balanced with projects that have created weapons of unimaginable destructive power. Projects that have delivered advanced in medicine have been balanced with projects which have destroyed ecosystems.

How does this apply to me achieving my goals?

So you may be thinking … well, how does this relate to me. How does this help me achieve my goals?

Well, first of all, this book is not intended to be a project management text book that walks you through all the techniques and intricacies of the vast world of project management. Consider this book a guide to the practical uses of project management in your daily life and its application to your specific goals, ideas, and dreams. It will walk you through all the steps necessary to achieving any goals you may have, and provide you with tools and resources to help you save time. The same techniques you will learn through this book have been used to achieve many of mankind's greatest modern achievements. You will be sharing in a long history of success.

The journey that you are beginning through the reading of this book embodies thousands of years of human achievement on a global level. It is my sincere hope that each and every reader of this book follows the steps, uses the tools, techniques and resources, and realizes for themselves the path to your dreams is a simple one. There is no secret or hidden knowledge here.

After walking with you through the basics steps of changing any aspect of your life that you wish to change, and providing you with the tools and guidance to plan for and work toward achieving your goals, you will have everything you need to transform your life into a life of "YOUR" choosing, a life you have designed and are happy to live in for the rest of your life.

Personal Retreat Workbook

THE BEGINNING OF A NEW LIFE

PERSONAL RETREAT

The idea of a retreat is nothing new. In fact, executives and management in corporations around the globe use corporate retreats as a tool to engage staff, develop new ideas, explore new goals, expand into new markets, and chart a path forward in this ever changing world. A personal retreat is an opportunity for you to take a step back from the world around you, find a quiet place away from all the things that remind you of the stresses in your life, and gather your thoughts to reconnect with yourself on a personal level. Most often, retreats are hosted in a hotel, spa retreat, cottage surrounded by nature, or other places where nobody can disturb the creative process. The most important thing for you to find with your personal retreat is a place where you will not be disturbed. Allowing yourself to remain focused on your activities will ensure the best outcomes. This could also be an opportunity for some quiet relaxation and alone time to de-stress. You could even make an event of it where you could reserve a hotel room at a spa or bed and breakfast, schedule some personal pampering time for you to relax and then begin the retreat exercises with a clear and unobstructed mind.

Once you have decided on when and where you will have your personal retreat, you will need to print a copy of the **Personal Retreat Workbook** before you go. The workbook will provide you with step by step guidance through the important journey you will take to develop your current life assessment and goals for the future.

Setting the Stage for a Change

There is no exact formula to delivering successful results within a personal or executive retreat, but there are things you can do to give yourself the opportunity to achieve a better outcome. Firstly, make sure to give yourself enough time. There is no deadline for completing this exercise, but there is a limited opportunity to ensure complete focus. The time allotted to your personal retreat should be adjusted to allow you to capture all the information you need to move forward, focus on you and redefine YOUR future. Some people can manage to complete this work in a few hours and others may take several weeks. Whatever time you set aside, your goal is to complete this work as comprehensively as possible.

Getting away from everything and everyone, and going to a place that is entirely new and that you have never been to before will help you relax and focus on the work of life redesign. If there are other people around or some form of distractions, try to find a secluded place where you will have total peace and quiet and will be undisturbed.

When you need a mental or physical break, engage in some pampering or relaxation services to de-stress and return focus back onto yourself. Enjoy a casual stroll, a nature walk, a coffee or glass of wine on a restaurant patio, and enjoy the company of your own thoughts.

Break Free - Brainstorming

Stop and look around. Look at where you are in your life NOW. Look at what has brought you here, reflecting on your past choices. Look at where you are headed if this pattern lasts forever. Consider different options, paths, or decisions you can make or take now and what the immediate potential consequences would be of making new choices. Start thinking about small changes you can make or ideas you can enable, to begin conceptualizing the future impact of those changes over a longer period of time. You can document your thoughts in the Personal Retreat Workbook as you go along. After you have thought about small changes, you can begin thinking about larger life changes and ideas you can enable to affect major life changes.

An example of a small change could be changing your hair color or your choice of daily breakfast. What would happen if you changed these small things in your life? What are potential good and unpleasant results of making these changes? Try to gage the impact severity of these choices. How would you feel? What would the costs be (not just monetary)? How would you be perceived by others? Document as much detail ask you can about how you see these small changes affecting your life in the short term and then over a long period of time.

Once you have completed this exercise for small changes, think about making larger changes to your life. An example of a large change could be quitting your job, moving to a new city or country, getting divorced or married, or buying a house. Following the same steps as with smaller changes, try your best to conceptualize and document the impact that making these large changes would have to your life. What are potential positive and negative results of making these changes? Try to gage the impact severity of these choices. How would you feel? How would you survive? What would the costs be (not just monetary)? How would you be perceived by others? Document as much detail ask you can about how you see these large changes affecting your life in the short term and then over a long period of time.

Don't be afraid to write down any and all ideas that come to mind during this process, as each will carry value and will be explored. This process of "Brainstorming" is typically used in groups to help think of new ways to solve problems or to promote creative thinking for the development of new ideas and approaches. Being totally honest with yourself in thinking about your current stage in life, and in what direction you would like your life to grow, is vital at this point in order to create good outcomes in future exercises. Use the Brainstorming pages to compose your thoughts and add pages if you need more space.

Step 1 - Self-Assessment

List what you consider to be all of the most important areas in your life. Once you have listed them, go through your list and reorder the items according to priority with the most important at the top and the least important at the bottom. Once complete, this list will identify your personal Key Life Areas.

List your current daily routine (typical day) in as much detail as possible, for one week day, and one weekend day.

Look at the lists side by side and identify connections between what you feel is most important in your life and what you do on a daily basis. Try to quantify the value of the items listed by time, effort, value, money, and whatever else you can use as a measure to identify how much the item is represented in your current daily routine. For example, if health and wellbeing is high on your list of Key Life Areas but your current daily schedule only has 30 minutes of exercise listed on a weekly basis, this would indicate a conflicting application of values.

The goal of this part of the exercise is to highlight how much of what you feel are the most important aspects of your life are reflected in your day to day routine, and identify areas where there is a perceived or real conflict in the values that you hold important, so they can be explored and resolved.

Step 2 – Find the time - Free up your time

From the previous section titled Common Knowledge, I identified 4 Key Areas including your work life, personal life, relationships, and physical wellbeing. These areas represent a large component of your day to day life and your overall happiness. The exercises we worked through together within that section will lay the foundation for this segment of your personal retreat.

Let us revisit what we have already learned in preparation for your personal retreat.

In your **Work Life**, you discovered to what degree your work life encroaches on your personal life and what retirement might look like for you.

In your **Personal Life**, you discovered how to find time in your schedule for your own personal endeavors and how sharing work with someone else enables a task to be completed in a shorter amount of time.

In your **Relationships**, you unplugged, rediscovered and reconnected with yourself and the important people in your life by carving out time in your schedule.

In your **Physical Health**, you learned how to begin applying the technique of principled living to plan and effortlessly automate the work needed to achieving your ideal health.

Now, to work toward any goal, you will need time: time to plan; time to connect with people; and, time to execute the work that will bring you closer to and eventually achieve your goal. Review the outcomes of your Work Life exercise on **work encroachment** and your Personal Life **finding the time** and identify 3-5 ways you can recapture at least 5 hours of your time each week (1 hour a day) to work on achieving your goals. On the page provided in your Personal Retreat Workbook, detail all of the different ways you have identified pockets of free time in your schedule, and the specific blocks of time that you have discovered by following the noted exercises. For each of the blocks of time you have identified, set a repeating calendar appointment with notification or reminders to reserve these times for your transformative work.

Step 3 – Defining your ideal life

Having completed the previous exercises should give you a clear picture of the current state of your life. You should also have an idea of the factors, people and events that have brought you to this point in your life, and what the possible impact might be of making small or large changes to aspects of your life going forward. You have conceptualized and worked through some exercises that are designed to help you think how changes you make would work, the impacts they may have immediately and over time, and the plausibility of them increasing or decreasing your level of happiness in the long run. Now you will take this exercise to the next level. You will be defining your ideal life, the life that currently lives in your dreams, and developing your custom list of goals that will capture the links between your current life and your dream life. This list of goals will be used to map out the path to get from where you are today to where you would like to be in your ideal state. Once completed, you can work at whatever pace you want on these goals, or even set them aside for a later time, but you will at least have a complete and clear understanding of where you are today and what your plans are for your future at this point in time. So let's begin defining your goals.

In your Personal Retreat Worksheet, you will begin documenting key aspects of your life as they are now and once complete, you will begin defining the same key aspect of your life in a way that captures the way you want it to be. For example, if I am currently 300 pounds, then I would put that figure under the physical health section of the template, and if I want to be 190 pounds at some future point, then I would place that figure beside my original weight in the ideal state column.

The Worksheet will guide you through a typical array of well-defined components that most people connect with in their lives and would like to see changes happen in. If there is a section that you feel you are totally happy with now, then just enter a positive word to describe your current state (like Happy, Fantastic, Wonderful, I ROCK, Goal Achieved, or whatever your like that is positive) and place the word ACCOMPLISHED in the future state field.

For any unique areas in your life that are not defined within the common template, I have included a custom template that is blank for you to capture these specific details of your life that you would like to see change and identify its current and future state. You could make as many copies of these templates as you wish to fully capture what you would like to see change in your life and write down the details. Also, as you begin to work through and complete some of your goals, you will undoubtedly think of new goals to work toward and more interesting projects to work on, to build on your previous successes. You can go back to these templates as your starting point and begin working through the process as many times as you wish in your lifetime to build on previous levels of happiness and keep capturing new stages in your life.

When you have complete all that you want to capture in your quest for your ideal life, then you will go through your list and rank the items by their level of importance to you. Level of importance is both a degree of urgency based on the value you place on that aspect of your life as well as when you want this change to occur, sooner or later. For example, if something is very important to you but is not so urgent that you need to start working on it today, then it will rank lower than something that is of equal importance and which you feel a burning need to start working on it now.

To the right of the Future state column, you will see three columns labeled Size, Value, and Time. In the column labelled Size, you will use one of three options to define how big a project or change that item represents in terms of amount of work and relative ease to incorporate into life. Now some small items will have a big impact on your life, but this column is about the level of effort you need to expend to work on achieving this goal. The three options are Small, Medium, and Large, which will help size the complexity of your project.

In the Value column, you will choose from 3 options, High, Medium, and Low. You will review each item listed in your template and place one of the three value options in the value field, with High being the most important aspect you would like to change, to Low being the least important item in relation to all the others on the list. Now I respect that all items that are on your list are important or else they would not be listed, but you are working through developing your priorities. As the saying goes, "when everything is a priority, then nothing is a priority". This exercise will give focus to your list.

After you have identified your High, Medium, and Low priorities, you will look to the column labelled Time and insert one of three options, Now (0-3 months), Later (3-9 months), Anytime (9 months or later). Remember that there is only one YOU and there are a limited number of hours in the day, so be careful when making your selection to choose options that when added together will represent a body of work that would need to be completed within your time schedule.

Once you have gone through your entire list, completing the Size, Value, and Time columns, you need to convert each descriptive word into a numeric value. Use the following legend to place the appropriate number beside each word.

Legend:

In the **Size** Column:

    Small   = 5   Medium   = 3   Large   = 1

In the **Value** Column:

    High   = 5   Medium   = 3   Low   = 1

In the **Time** Column:

    Now   = 5   Later   = 3   Anytime   = 1

After you have completed adding the numeric value next to each descriptive word in the three columns, it is time to add up the values. For each row, add the numeric values for Size, Value, and Time, and enter the value into the Total field. Go through the list and repeat the same for each row. In the end, every row will have a value in the Total field. The values in the Total field represent the items that are most important to you, prioritized by when you want to begin working on them and their relative size from smallest and easiest to largest and most complex.

This exercise is designed to be a simple representation of a ranking exercise and there are many ways to complete this exercise, so if you feel you can arrive at a ranked list of what is important to you by using a different method, then please feel free to use whatever approach feels comfortable.

Complete List Method of Ranking

At this stage in the ranking process there are two ways forward. You can look at the entire list of ranked items, take all of the numeric values that are the same and add a letter to each one starting from A to further rank values that the same numeric rank, so that in the end you will have a completely ranked list of goals, irrespective of size, that is ranked by importance to you.

Complete List Method:

Life Area	Current	Future	Size	Value	Time	Total	Final Rank
Health	Weight 300lbs	Weight 190lbs	Large (1)	High (5)	Now (5)	11	3
Finance	$15/hr job	$30/hr job	Small (5)	Medium (3)	Now (5)	13A	1
Relationship	Unattached	Married	Large (1)	Medium (3)	Anytime (1)	5	5
Spirituality	Lost	Found	Small (5)	High (5)	Later (3)	13B	2
Travel	Been Nowhere	See Europe	Medium (3)	Medium (3)	Later (3)	9	4

Size Group Method of Ranking

The alternate method is to group all of the projects by size first (grouping all of the small projects, then the medium projects and then the large projects), and then within each size group, ranking each goal by total of the Value and Time columns alone. Then you can look at the each size group, take all of the numeric values that are the same and add a letter to each one starting from A to further rank the duplicates, so that in the end you will have a completely ranked list of goals, grouped by size, and that is ranked by importance to you.

Size Group Method:

Life Area	Current	Future	Size	Value	Time	Total	Final Rank
SMALL							
Finance	$15/hr job	$30/hr job	Small (5)	Medium (3)	Now (5)	8A	2
Spirituality	Lost	Found	Small (5)	High (5)	Later (3)	8B	3
MEDIUM							
Travel	Been Nowhere	See Europe	Medium (3)	Medium (3)	Later (3)	6	4
LARGE							
Health	Weight 300lbs	Weight 190lbs	Large (1)	High (5)	Now (5)	10	1
Relationship	Unattached	Married	Large (1)	Medium (3)	Anytime (1)	4	5

At the end of the Complete List method or the Size Group method, rank the total column from largest to smallest number (taking into account the letter sub-rankings starting at A) and place the value in the Final Rank field. Generally speaking, these two approaches are designed to capture two different types of people. Those who are comfortable with what has been described so far and who feel capable of handling the most difficult and challenging tasks first would use the Complete List Method to move forward to the next stage of the process, whereas those who just want to work through simple and small projects first and then tackle larger and more complex projects when they feel more comfortable, should use the Size Group Method to move forward. At this point, by breaking down, defining and ranking by importance the areas of your life that you feel need some change, you should at least feel a bit more comfortable with the idea that it is not an insurmountable task that you can never manage to achieve. After all, as they say, "The best way to eat an elephant is one bite at a time." (Creighton Abrams)

Now that you have completed defining the gap between aspects of your current life in relation to what you envision would be your ideal life, you can begin to bridge these gaps and detail how you plan to get from where you are now to where you want to be in the future. But before you can move to this stage, I would encourage you to complete Step 4 of this process, which is a vital component to the process of any kind of change.

Step 4 – Commit to change one thing that is important to you

Many people will tell you that if you want to change your life, you have to do everything all at once, that there is no time to lose, and that you have to expend a lot of effort. Like a fitness instructor trying to run you into the ground in your first class or smack the fat off of you over the span of a month through a boot-camp mentality, this approach breaks the spirit and is not always sustainable in the long term. I am letting you know right now that this approach is a total bunch of lies! Any aspect of life change is a gradual and consistent process that starts small, and over time transforms that changing aspect into something totally different and wonderful. Like water transforms jagged rocks into smooth pebbles over time through a consistent flow of current, making small seemingly effortless adjustments in your life will transform it into a totally different life over time. Remember that you are mapping out and creating a new path, and allowing the waters of change to flow on your new path to achieve your goals. We pace ourselves to what we are comfortable with and over time build momentum to achieve our goals with relative ease. Just like resolving yourself to dropping your loose change into a jar whenever you pass it. Over time the jar becomes full without you even realizing it. A simple small change leads us to a great amount of change, if you catch my meaning.

So at this point in your reading of this book, all I would like you to do is make a commitment to yourself, not to me, not to anyone else, but to yourself, that you will choose ONE thing that is important to you that you would like to see change in your life, and commit to changing that thing into what you envision that thing being at its best for you. After all, any serious attempt at life change cannot be done while sitting on the fence or watching from the sidelines. One must make a decision, choose a path forward, fully commit, and make their own dreams come true. When you make your commitment, do so consciously knowing that a commitment is the deepest essence of who we are as individuals. It is a solemn promise to our own true self that we will execute our free will to perform an action or pursue a result unobstructed by any opposing force. We have worked through the self-assessment exercise together, shifted the focus back onto you, helped you think about the things that matter most to you, and helped you understand how you can find the time and resources needed to follow through with any number of changes you wish to make. Making a commitment to yourself means that you will do your very best to stay focused on what you want to change on a daily basis and to keep in mind the simple steps, outlines, and rules you set for yourself during times that you interact with events that affect your goal. This is about YOU, so be true to yourself and make that promise, that commitment to yourself that you will change at least one thing that is important to your life starting today. Write down your commitment on the template in as much detail as possible.

Step 5 – Find the Resources – Line 'em up!

As much as we may think we can do it all ourselves, everyone has limits. And if you have big dreams, recruiting help is the way to go. During the exercises in the above section on your **Personal Life**, you discovered how sharing work with someone else enables a task to be completed in a shorter amount of time. Projects always have a team with special skills that are needed to work toward the end goal. Now that you have identified your goals, you will begin to identify all the resources in your life now that can help you achieve your goals and identify gaps that need to be filled as well. For each major goal, you will also identify a mentor or someone that has personally completed a similar goal in their lives. Having someone to emulate, use as a sounding board, talk to candidly, get advice from, and just be yourself with is an invaluable asset when pursuing any goal. Mentors will not have all the answers and would have completed their goals under different circumstances and environments, however they would be able to offer a wonderful perspective on strategies you can employ, resources you could engage, and techniques you can use that will save you time and effort in achieving your similar goal.

Review your ranked list of goals and with your current network of connections in mind, work through each goal listed and link all the names of people that come to mind that you feel would be helpful in achieving each goal. When you work through this process, you may have names appearing in multiple places, and other areas where you have gaps. This is ok. Once you have made a complete first pass at your list, start from the top again looking at each item and adding to each list of names, the resources you will need to complete the project. They may not even be names, but could be a description of a resource like, lawyer, accountant, fitness instructor, realtor, or any other resource needed to ensure you reach that goal. Finally, match up the names of the resources you listed with the needed resources and identify which resources you are currently missing.

At this point, you will know what resources are needed to achieve your goals and the resources you currently have access to. Make a plan to connect with the people you have identified to fill them in on what you are doing and determine if they can provide the help you are looking for. Take some time beforehand to develop a compelling set of discussion points so that you make the most of your effort at reaching out. After you have completed reaching out to all of your known resources, you would begin your search to fill in the resource gaps, through your current network of colleagues, family, friends, acquaintances, or other available resources. Resource gaps would be the areas in which you have identified the need for a resource but have not identified a specific person to fill that need. Although a direct referral from someone you know personally is best, there are many resources both private and public that you can access to search for resources so carefully begin to fill in the gaps with contact information (including a few different choices when needed) until your list is complete with no gaps.

Step 6 – Drawing your roadmap - Decide what you want to change first

Like any journey, we all have to start somewhere. In your journey, you have tried to identify your personal starting point through the self-assessment exercises. This was intended to capture where you are as of today in key aspects of your life. Any effort to change the items listed within the self-assessment, now have a point of reference. Throughout the remainder of this book, I will be walking you through a detailed step by step approach to defining your goals, breaking down your goals, planning the work that is needed to take you from where you are now to where you want to be in the future, executing your plan, lining up needed resources, monitoring progress, and seeing the fruits of your plan develop into the achievement of your goals. Because the information will be new to you, and because I really want you to understand the whole process as we go along so that you can become familiar with applying it over and over to achieve other goals, I would like you to work through your list of goals from the self-assessment exercises to form your roadmap to life change.

As you work through the first goal on your list (the one you have committed to yourself to achieve), through the remainder of this book, you will be able to envision the process as it applies to other goals on your list, which will help you build your plans for those goals when the time is right. Beginning with a goal that is manageable and that will help you understand a process that will be applied over and over again, will give you confidence in your own ability to successfully plan and reach your life changing goals. Each goal will build on one another and when you are comfortable with the process, you will be able to start managing multiple projects at the same time to rapidly transform your life into what is ideal for you. Not all projects will succeed the first time around, and some will be stopped without being completed because the time was not right or some resources were not available to do all the needed work. There will always be things that you cannot predict, as life itself is unpredictable, but I will show you how to best account for these uncertainties and keep moving forward.

At the end of this book, you will know that you have the tools to transform your life and are well on your way to building and living the life you always dreamed of.

Part II

Bare Bones Project Management

Revealing the Wizard

To put it plainly, Project Management is just an organized way of getting things done to achieve something specific in a set amount of time. Within this book, the word project will be used interchangeably with the word goal or dream. Once you begin to use some of the techniques and processes laid out in this book, you will begin to realize that dreams are really better defined as goals because of the way project management tools can help you break them down into manageable parts and achieve them. Dreams are goals that are placed on pedestals because they feel like they are out of reach. Project Management tools provide you with a way to achieve these dreams, so they are no longer this fantasy or long shot. It is a reality that can be worked toward and achieved. So there is no need to be afraid of project management or think it is something you will not understand. I am here to walk you through it step by step in this section. Understanding the concept of project management is quite simple by using this 7 step process.

1) Identify and define what you want to accomplish (your goal or project scope)
2) Plan the work you need to do to reach your goal
   o List tasks and how long each will take to complete
   o Sequence your tasks
   o Develop a schedule
   o Identify the resources you will need and line them up
   o Identify the costs involved
3) Start managing the work according to your plan
   o Monitor the progress of the work in relation to your plan
   o Handle issues and problems as they arise
   o Make any changes or adjustments needed to your plan to keep moving forward
4) Communicate with your team to keep everyone informed
5) Finish all the work needed to achieve your goal
6) Check to make sure the goal has been achieved as defined
7) Close the project

By the end of this section, you will have a well-defined project that captures at least one of the goals in your Life Change list and the knowledge to fully complete the project from start to finish. So let us begin by developing a clearly defined SCOPE.

Scope Development

Defining the scope of your project is one of the most important aspects of a project. Capturing a detailed idea or picture of what you are trying to accomplish, create, or build. Spending the time to create the most detailed scope will make every other aspect of project planning and work that much easier later on during execution of the project. For example, if a child asks their parents for a red mountain bike for Christmas and the parents buy them a blue ten speed bike, Santa is sure to get an earful next Christmas, and the parents should expect to hear about it throughout the course of the next 365 days. Delivering what is expected, by referencing the scope statement throughout the project, is vital. The scope is your target and straying from it will cause the project to fail.

Many projects start with a goal or project objective that is obscure and that lacks specific information. When thinking about how a team or person could accomplish this obscure project outcome, there could be a very broad and multifaceted range of options for completing the project. The planning process is not just centered on finding any way to accomplish a project outcome; it is focused on the **most effective way** of completing the project to achieve the desired outcome. The idea that the process of running a project should be as effective and efficient as possible helps a PM choose a specific path for completing the project, and even filters down to the tasks involved and how they are completed. For example, on a project where the budget is small but the timeline to complete it is flexible and can be long, these factors will affect the way in which the project is managed. If there are expensive options and inexpensive options, then your choice is guided by the budget, and if time is a factor, your flexibility in timeline will also provide guidance.

Asking Questions is the Key

For obscure goals, the process of planning gives the PM and project team an opportunity to ask questions and refine the scope of the project to solidify aspects of the project that are not clear at the beginning. For example, a common personal goal of many people is to lose weight. This is an obscure goal because there are many aspects of this goal that can be defined clearly, yet are not currently defined. Asking questions is the key to help us better define the scope of this project, such as:

- How much weight do you want to lose?

- How much time do you want to devote to achieving this goal?

- What approach is preferred to achieving the goal, which could include: diet alone; exercise alone; a mix of diet and exercise; surgery; acupuncture; pills; other lifestyle changes; etc.?

- Has this project been attempted before and what was the outcome? What can be learned from previous attempts, previous successes, and previous failures?

- What resources are available to complete this goal? People, Money, Time?

- Is there a mentor that can help provide you with guidance and support?

The answers to these questions may look like this:

I want to lose 25 pounds in 6 months so that I can look fabulous at my class reunion. I do not have a specific budget in mind but I want to focus on exercise and diet adjustments to accomplish my goal. I have lost and gained weight in the past, gaining weight during extremely stressful times in my life. I have lots of friends and a solid supportive family. My cousin Mike has lost weight and kept it off for a long time. He has offered to be my mentor through this journey.

Scope Definition Worksheet

The result of our questioning has provided important information needed to plan out our project, specifically:

Weight Loss Goal:	25 pounds
Timeframe:	6 months
Reason:	Look good for class reunion
Budget:	Any
Specific Method:	Preference to Exercise and Eating adjustments
History:	High Stress has led to weight gain in the past
Resources:	Strong support system of friends and family, my doctor, resident nutritionist/personal trainer at my local gym.
Mentor:	My cousin Mike

Defining your goal or project scope may also include limitations to the outcome, or what is not included within the scope (**Out of Scope**). This becomes important in larger and more complex projects that involve several external resources, and that may need to have relationships for the completion of project work formalized through the use of contracts. For instance, if your goal is to build a house for your family and you hire specific trades to complete components of the project, and you have in mind to complete other specific parts of the project yourself, such as interior finishes, painting, etc., then this should be clearly defined in the contract with your trades. Should one of your contractors approach you at a later date asking you to pay for interior painting of some rooms within the house, you can clearly indicate that this component is excluded from the project work assigned to the contractor. Defining both what is included, and what is not included within a project scope, serves to paint a complete picture of your project and protects you from the potential for unscrupulous business practices from members of your project team.

Filling in the Blanks

Some additional things you can do to fill in some gray areas, using the same example as above, may include:

- **Consulting an Expert** – contacting experts in nutrition and exercise to find out what would work best for the person wishing to lose weight will provide valuable information on options. When connecting with experts, remember to ask them about their own experiences with weight gain and loss to ensure they have first-hand personal experience in the work required to accomplish the goal.

- **Independent Research** – you can perform independent research on methods of weight loss, however as with any resource that you talk to or anything that you read in books or online, it is important to ensure the information is not misinformation or outright lies! Any information on the internet is not vetted for accuracy and any incomplete media accounts should be questioned as well. It is always better to connect with individuals directly without any intermediaries, and specifically search out people who have had first-hand experience with achieving a similar goal as you have outlined. This means, if you are looking to lose 100 pounds, call your local gym, speak to your family doctor, and reach out to friends in search for someone else who has personally lost the same or more weight and kept it off so that you can ask them how they did it.

- **First Hand Account** – For almost every personal project, there is someone out there that has had first-hand experience achieving it or achieving a component of it. Broadening your network in search of friends, people with common goals, and potential mentors with first-hand experience with goal you are looking to accomplish is an ongoing process and will take time. Don't let that stop you from continuing the journey you are on, just keep this in mind as you strive for achievement in your life as people naturally gravitate to those willing to tempt fate to transform their lives. Actively searching for people with first hand is also easier in this wonderfully connected world.

Whether you are looking to build a billion dollar business, lose weight, change careers, expand your family, or rebuild your life after a tragedy, do some research to identify local resources in your city or region and reach out to schedule a meeting or phone call. Of course this is putting your faith in people, but in my experience, when approached nicely and in a respectful way, people of all stages of success in their lives are willing to talk about their experiences. Be patient and respectful when you are making any request, ask with clear intention, and follow-up with kindly reminders. Remember that it may take some time to schedule you into their busy calendar, but if your approach is genuine and you ask with a kind respect, you may have an opportunity afforded to very few people. If you are granted a meeting, make sure you prepare yourself in advance and be concise with your points so that the person you are meeting feels like their time is being valued. You could also be creative in your approach by letting the person know that you are writing an article about a certain topic and would like to include their personal experiences as reference to the specific topic. If you are going to use this approach, follow through with your claim, write, and publish an article online. Also, send the individual a copy of the link to the article so that they know you are a person of upstanding character, and worthy of a follow-up conversation. Whether working on complex or simple projects, connecting with people that have done similar things in their own personal and professional lives can be an invaluable resource, and having them available as a mentor, sounding board, or just someone to talk to can be extremely valuable. So take the time to connect with people throughout your scoping and planning phases and keep their information documented so that you can communicate at regular intervals on the status of your project.

- **Informed Guess** - Take an informed guess at what you believe the grey area would look like. Doing research on gray areas and talking to people who have shared their experiences are a wonderful start, but they might not exactly capture the specifics of gray areas within your project. It is up to you to interpret the information that applies to your project and capture the relevant information that is useful or could impact project success. Taking an informed guess and documenting it will be useful during project planning and can be revisited and revised during the work phase of the project, to incorporate actual results, events, knowledge, or experience. Do your best to define the gray areas so that you first of all realize they exist, and secondly are able to incorporate them into your plan as an opportunity and/or a risk.

With all of the information you have explored in this section, use the Scope Definition Worksheet to document the specifics of the project scope for the project or series of projects you have chosen to achieve throughout the remainder of our journey. If you intend on working toward the achievement of more than one dream at this time, then you will need to complete documentation for each specific goal from this point forward. Remember to keep all your information in a binder, workbook, or computer file folder for easy organization and reference.

Be "SMART" About your Scope

SMART is a principle used to help fully capture the scope of your goal (dream) and to ensure you have thought about essential requirements to define and conceptualize key aspects in preparation for planning your project to achieve your dream. For each project you design, using the SMART approach will ensure your scope is well defined and has enough information to create a good plan for achievement. Start with the first item in your ranked Life Change list, and work through this approach to help you create a statement that will fully capture your project scope. Using the templates available will help you keep your thoughts well organized and will ensure all the information needed is completed throughout this process. Questions which are asked in the dialogue below will be repeated in the templates. To begin, look at the top ranked goal on your list and write a detailed statement that defines every detail of your ideal future state. Once you have fully defined in great detail what you intend to achieve at the completion of your project, you can begin assessing your project scope using the SMART principle to make sure you have all the information needed to develop a fantastic project plan. (Doran, G. T. (1981). "There's a S.M.A.R.T. way to write management's goals and objectives". Management Review (AMA FORUM) 70 (11): 35–36.)

The SMART Principle can be broken down as follows:

S – Specific

Being specific about what you want to achieve, build, or create is a vital first step in the success of your project. Define your idea being as specific as possible. Outline every aspect of what you want to do and what will you accomplish by implementing your idea. It should be a clear image in your mind and like painting a picture should be described as if it were a reality standing right in front of you. If there are any areas that are grey or unknown about what you are looking to do or achieve, now is the time to talk to people. For whatever dream you have, there are always people who have achieved that same or similar goals and who are happy to talk to you. It may take a few calls, but there are no secrets here. You would be surprised at how happy and willing successful people are to talk to other people about their lives and their accomplishments. You just need to reach out, explain what you are looking for in a respectful manner and ask nicely for their help in understanding what is involved. And if someone gives you a hard time, move on to the next person and don't take it personally. It's as simple as that. At the end of this step, you should have a detailed image of what the outcome of your project should look like.

M – Measurable

Measuring your progress to achieving success in anything over a period of time requires landmarks along the way. You need to define what landmarks are on the road you are travelling, that will indicate that you are either on the right path or travelling in the right direction to reach your goal. When you arrive at these landmarks, you should be more confident that you are doing the right thing. If you are not reaching the measurable results you have planned at the times you expected, it is a sign that you need to take a closer look at what is going on, identify any barriers that are preventing you moving in the right direction according to plan, and adjust your plan to get you back on track. Measures of success are the tangible aspects of your project that you can define and track your progress against. Ask yourself, how will you know when you have accomplished your goal? What are the measures of success? Identify targets to achieve by a certain time. Some projects set measures at certain levels of completion such as 25% complete, 50% complete, and so on. You must be very careful with measuring progress in this way, especially if there is someone providing a paid service to you or are receiving money in exchange for a component of your project to be completed within a specific timeframe. Unless your relationship is defined in a contract specifying the expectation that all work will be completed by a given date, and that your final payment to them will be held until the final work is complete, then they are in a position to continue billing you for their own delay. Providing additional time to a specific task being completed by someone else is also a difficult situation as work has a tendency to fill up all available time assigned to a task. If you think a resource will have time left over to complete additional work within a window of time you have provided for minimal work, don't count on it. The principal defining this practice is called Parkinson's Law which simply states "work expands so as to fill the time available for its completion".

Measures are control mechanisms that alert you to progress within your project and the work you have assigned to other resources, and provide feedback to give you time to make plan adjustments. Good results are demonstrated through achieving a measurable target while saving time, reduced cost, or achieving more than expected within the timeframe provided (i.e. more value). Bad results may include a failure to achieve the measurable target outcome, spending more time than budgeted for on a task or finding a cost increase for an unforeseen item or event. Good or bad, feedback should always been seen as a positive thing and defining measurable outcomes along your planned path is an important tool in the planning process.

A – Achievable

Is your goal achievable and what steps are you planning to take to achieve that goal? This is the focus of this step. Create a step by step list of all the ways possible that you can achieve your goal. This is where out of the box thinking is helpful. Also, you can tap other people for this as well by asking them what they did to achieve a similar goal, or even a portion of a goal. Using lessons that other people have learned about their successes and even their failures can provide useful insight into planning all of the possibilities available to achieving a goal. Remember that this is not a process of identifying a single path toward achieving your goal. This step involves brainstorming and documenting EVERY path you can possibly think of to achieving your goal.

Be creative and outline all the paths you think are available. Take note that these steps are in a specific order of thinking and you should only think about the steps in their given order. To complete this step, you should not limit your list of ways to achieve a given goal by the resources needed or available, or limit your scope in step one by what you feel are limitations to what you are capable of. Open yourself up to the infinite possibilities, as this is capturing dreams without limits. If a path requires specific resources, list those resources and plan as if they are present. Also, do not limit your planning to your own creativity. Talk to people. Get their take on how they would achieve the specific goal. Just make sure the people you approach have first-hand experience achieving a similar goal or at least a portion of the goal. For example, if a dream you are outlining carries a component requiring the raising of $500,000 in capital and you have no clue on how to achieve this, talking to a banker, an investment advisor, a private investor, or successful business owner may provide you with ideas you have never thought of or experienced before. Their insight can turn a project from a pipe dream into a plausible reality. I truly believe that every dream is achievable. The challenge is achieving a dream within a set budget, timeline, and with available resources. Dream big and prove to yourself, through the achievement of smaller goals first before tackling larger goals, that you are able to achieve great things.

R – Realistic

This is the step where you place your dream into a box that defines how long you will work on this dream, what resources are available to you, and how realistic achieving your goal is as defined. Can this goal be achieved given the current availability of resources, knowledge, and time? Identify the resources needed, budget, people, products, and stakeholders within this step. A stakeholder is basically anyone with an interest in, an impact on, or who will be impacted by your project effort or outcome. When you give your goals a lot of time to be achieved, there are positive techniques available and also challenges to contend with. The challenges are running out of resources, losing focus on the specific goal or path to achieving the goal, or going through too many re-planning cycles so as to have your goal essentially look entirely different than what you originally defined. As a rule of thumb, try to keep your projects less than two years in length so that you have sufficient time to demonstrate progress and achieve outcomes while keeping your focus razor sharp. If you have a project that will take longer than 2 years, break it up into more than one project and manage them consecutively. Another aspect of a longer project timeframe is the grey area that encompasses future uncertainty. This could be both good and bad and should be managed as a risk, however if you do your research and develop a keen knowledge of the components necessary to complete your project, it could be very positive. Industries that consistently practice planning for technology that does not exist into projects with long timelines, during the planning and development of new products; include the aerospace industry and the motion picture industry. Both industries must be at the cutting edge of technology to remain competitive and attract the attention of their consumers, so they continually incorporate emerging technologies and resources into their projects and plan for the future reality of those components being in existence at the time they are needed for their projects. This just goes to demonstrate that we all take risks in the projects we design and work on to achieve our dreams, but that knowledge and experience guides us to what is plausible and realistic.

Resources:

Being realistic about your project also means taking account of your available resources. Remember that you have been creative in identifying resources, but now is the time to take stock of what your reality looks like at this point in time. Reach out to identify what resources are actually available from your list of needed resources to complete your project. Identify gaps in key resources and consult all possible resources and people within your network to see how you can fill the gaps and if needed, the cost of doing so. Having missing resources does not necessarily mean your project should be shelved. What it means is that you need help lining them up and may have to adjust your project schedule and budget to get the project going. It is an exercise in creative thinking and connecting with people that you are more than capable of successfully completing.

Budget:

As with recruitment of resources, your budget is another constraint because it is a predetermined fixed value. All projects have limited resources and money is one of the key resources that can determine the success or failure of a project. Be realistic about exploring all paths to successfully complete your project and for each one you are seriously exploring, determine what the budget would be and where the budget would be allocated. Your time must also be factored into the equation as well, because your effort represents a value to the project. Make sure it is represented by a monetary figure, as if you are completing the project for someone else, with you as a paid Project Manager. Again, you can develop your creative juices to reduce the actual costs involved as you get closer to launching your project, but you need at a minimum to capture the value of effort in this step so that you can be realistic when asking other people to sacrifice their time or contribute in some way.

T – Time Based

This final step in your SMART assessment is applying a timeline to achieving the scope of your goal. No project lasts forever and, as explained earlier, long projects promote the loss of focus and are very difficult to plan with any level of accuracy. Placing a timeline on your project allows you to define resources and the duration of tasks to work within the timeframe. Time is one of the components of your **Iron Triangle** (which will be explained shortly) which means extending or decreasing the amount of time to complete a project will allow you to resize other areas including project cost, quality, and scope. If your scope is too large to develop a reasonable timeframe, then redefining your scope into multiple sequential projects can help keep the timeframe within a reasonable range. When thinking about completing this step, ask yourself the question; when will the goal be accomplished? Reflect on all the other steps you have taken, all the people you have spoken to, and all the knowledge you have gained to this point in defining the time you are allowing for completing your project. Make sure it's an informed figure and not just an unrealistic number of months or a broadly undefined value of "however long it takes". Define it, plan for it, and work toward it.

<u>SMART Template</u>

Scope Statement

Defining what a project will achieve in detail is an essential component to project success. At this point you have documented the scope of your project and refined your scope by using the SMART process. Now it is time to solidify all this information into a single document that will be your single reference point throughout the planning and running of your project. The document is typically called a Scope Statement and it is a precise and complete representation of what you will be working to achieve. It will also be important in the final stages of your project as it will be referred to in your final check to determine if your objectives have been fully met.

<u>Scope Statement Worksheet</u>

Additional Scoping Concepts

Your Goal is SMART … now what?

At this point, you have used the SMART principle to add necessary detail to fully define your project scope. You have a clear understanding of what you would like to accomplish at the end of the project you will be designing. This level of detail should help keep you focused and excited throughout the remainder of the project planning process. But before you jump into planning, there are two simple yet important concepts that will be useful to you during the planning process. These concepts will be of great help in conceptualizing two key areas within the process: Resources and Interdependent Connections.

Hierarchy of Needs

In the year 1943, a gentleman by the name of Abraham Maslow proposed a theory which is now termed "Maslow's Hierarchy of Needs", which simply states that each of us is motivated by an instinctive and natural set of needs, from basic physiological needs to needs that serve to satisfy the realization of higher goals to reach ones full personal potential. Although this theory is controversial, it is still widely used to demonstrate concepts surrounding our individual motivations. I raise this theory here for two reasons; firstly, to show that there is a connection between all these needs, and that lower needs facilitate higher needs, by affording us the opportunity to focus on them from the comfort of an environment where basic needs are being met; and secondly, to highlight that some needs can only be accomplished through your own will, and even with the guidance of other people or resources, the ultimate source of change needs to come from within. Leading into the planning process, it is important to properly characterize your projects as internal or external so that you can plan resources and your level of effort accordingly, and also to make sure the environment in which your project will be completed meets all the required needs to achieve project success.

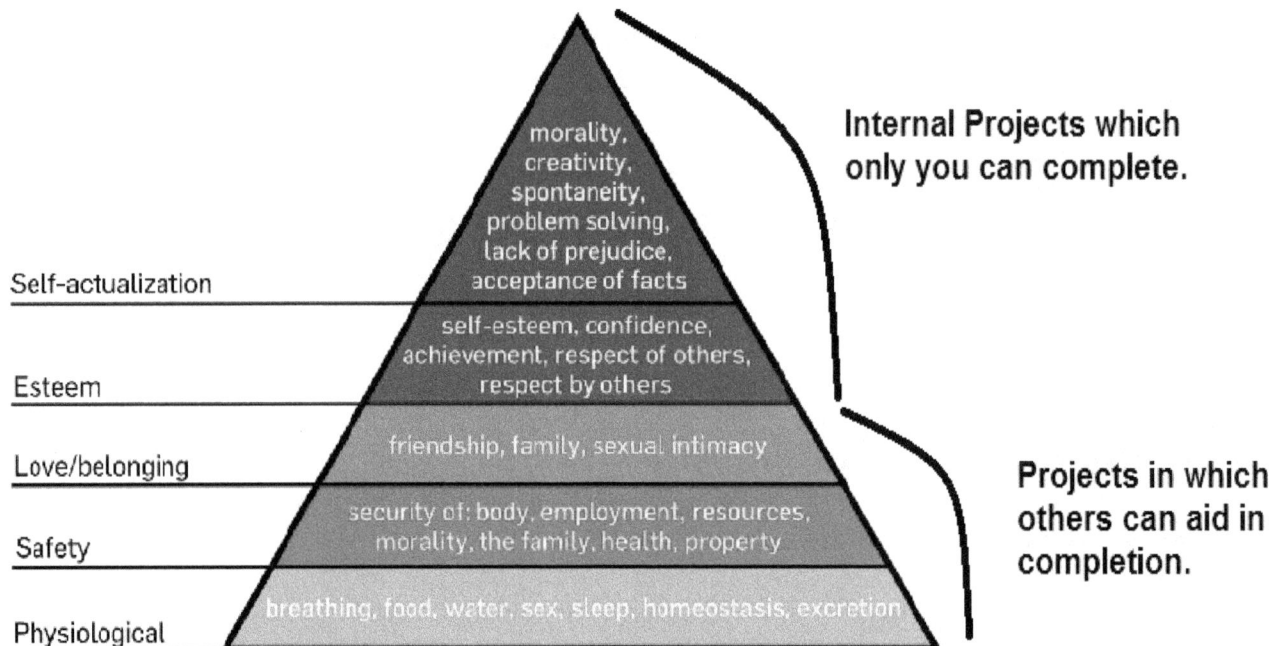

Internal Projects which only you can complete.

Projects in which others can aid in completion.

Maslow's Hierarchy of Needs:

- **Self-actualization**: morality, creativity, spontaneity, problem solving, lack of prejudice, acceptance of facts
- **Esteem**: self-esteem, confidence, achievement, respect of others, respect by others
- **Love/belonging**: friendship, family, sexual intimacy
- **Safety**: security of: body, employment, resources, morality, the family, health, property
- **Physiological**: breathing, food, water, sex, sleep, homeostasis, excretion

Project Management's Iron Triangle

Going by a variety of names, the Project Management Triangle or Iron Triangle is a visual tool that highlights the interdependent relationship between the three key constraints within a project (triple constraint), being Time, Cost, and Scope (or sometimes combined with Quality). What it is designed to demonstrate firstly is the key constraints of a project, as they are the essence of the key components of a project, and secondly that changing one of these constraints will have an impact on at least one or both of the other constraints and that at the point of change, the project team should be reminded to explore other necessary changes to keep the project viable.

Two example of this are as follows:

If a scope has been established at the onset of a project and a change to the scope is made later, there is a high probability that additional time or cost would be needed to account for any rework, adjustments to the project plan, or sourcing of different resources, materials, or products.

One technique used on occasion to complete a project faster than originally planned is called "Crashing" the schedule, which could involve adding more resources to complete tasks quicker. This can have a positive impact on Time, however the additional resources come at a cost which will affect the overall project Cost, and having too many resources can cause challenges in coordination, overlapping work and other inefficiencies which may negatively impact the Scope/Quality.

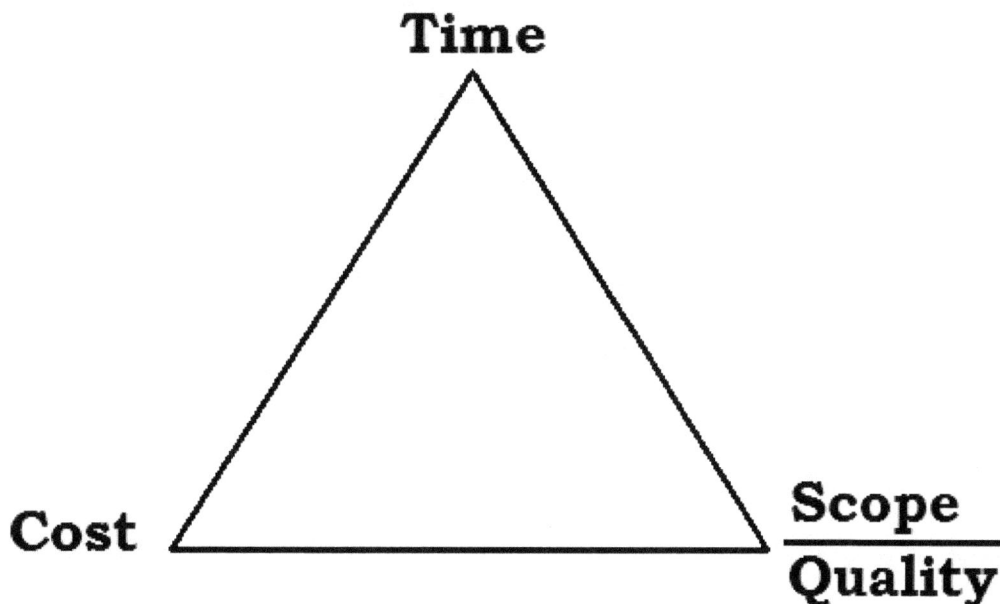

Time

Cost

Scope

Quality

Both Maslow's Hierarchy of Needs and the Iron Triangle are tools to help you think about the environment in which you are running your project, the forces that are at play that may impact your project, and interdependent relationships within different areas of your project, which are important to envision as you enter the planning phase.

Plan, Do, Check, Act

Now that you have defined the scope of your goal (dream) and gone through the steps to ensure your scope is SMART, you can begin the cycles of project management and project work that will lead to achieving your goal. While project work can be seen as linear in that sequential, consecutive or concurrent tasks are completed to work through a plan to complete the overall project, and that when all tasks are complete the project is complete, the project management process itself is cyclical. The reason for this is to allow us to plan work and receive continuous feedback to assess the quality and progress of the work being completed so that we can make adjustments and course corrections to arrive at the ideal outcome. This cycle is necessary to account for real events as a project is running, and unforeseen issues that inevitably arise in all projects that have a relative impact on project work or the project itself. Sometimes this will involve adjusting your plan, adding or deleting tasks, redefining your scope, or modifying your budget. Projects should be looked at as living breathing organisms with many moving parts and many influences. Keeping a close eye on your project by following this cycle will help keep you on track to achieve the project outcome as close to your plan as possible.

Project management has been around for a long time, as demonstrated in part by achievements going back to ancient times. Remnants of ancient cultures, archeological findings, and architectural wonders that continue to exist today reveal that the planning and coordination of human effort needed to create these extraordinary feats of engineering and artistic creation existed in some form during those times. As with most established professions, Project Management has refined itself and looked beyond its beginnings to incorporate useful tools from other professions and streams of thought. The cycle I will focus on here can be termed a few different ways but is essentially the same structure which is used in project management, lean management, manufacturing, computer software development, quality programs, and many more fields of work. In project management, the cycle is called IPDCAdC which stands for Initiate, Plan, Do, Check, Adapt, and Close which can also be stated as the five stages of project management being Initiation, Planning, Execution, Monitoring & Control, and Close.

The five stages of project management can be visually described like this:

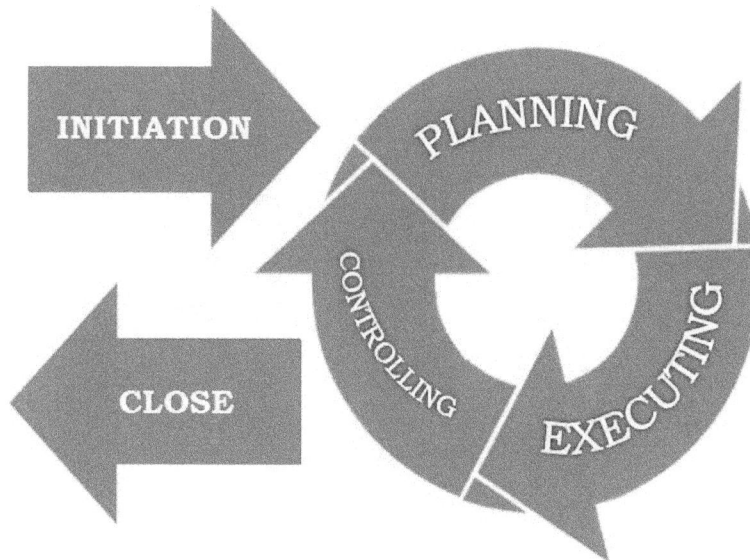

This cycle is a slight adaptation of a cycle called PDCA developed by Walter Shewhart and refined by Edward Deming which focusses on the core elements of Planning, Doing, Checking, and Acting/Adjusting. The Plan, Do, Check, Act cycle is most commonly used in Continuous Improvement efforts to minimize variation in an end product through constant review, learning, monitoring and incorporation of what has been learned back into the process.

The PDCA cycle is a wonderful start for someone new to project management because it encourages observation, learning, and application of new learning back into the planning process. The goal is eliminating waste and/or wasted effort so working through this cycle will make you and your team more efficient in their work, and as you continue developing and managing other projects to transform your life, your skills and results will increase exponentially.

PDCA is an easy to remember cycle that you would incorporate in many different ways in your projects. First within the overall project effort, from planning the project (PLAN), through execution of the project tasks (DO), to monitoring the outcomes of the activities (CHECK), to adjusting your approach and/or your plan to incorporate what you have learned and to get closer and closer to achieving the result you planned for (ACT).

Again, the steps in the cycle are as follows:

- Plan – Plan the work
- Do – Execute the plan
- Check – Check to see if your actual results are heading in the right direction to get to the end product or expected outcome
- Act (or Adjust) – make modifications to the plan or project to put it back on course to achieve the goal

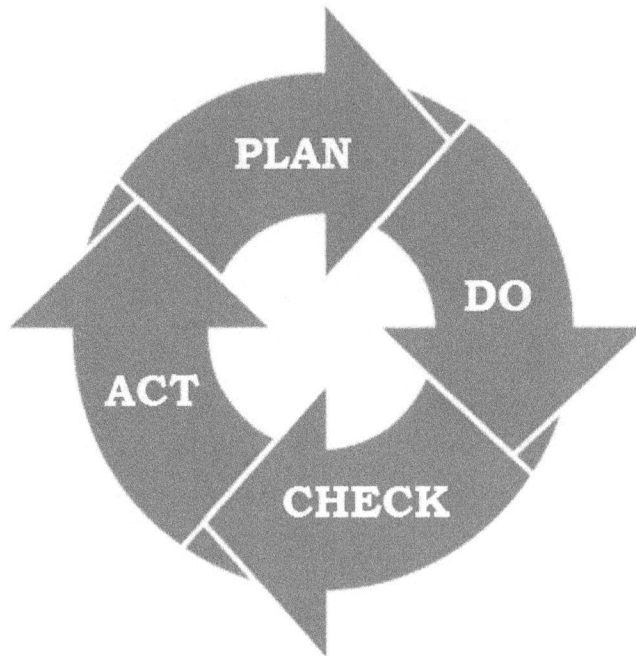

Once a project is initiated and has a documented scope, it enters the planning phase of the cycle. On completion of initial project planning, execution of the work begins and the project manager and team begin controlling and monitoring the completion of project related tasks. A check is performed at the completion of each task or major group of tasks to see if the result of task completion meets the expected outcome. Management of issues related to task completion is also done at this stage, to provide guidance to the project team and to help facilitate their work. At this stage when the project manager is seeing work being completed, elements in the project that were loosely defined or gray at the start of the project may begin to become more apparent or solid. When this happens, the cycle returns to the planning phase so that new information and actual results from the execution phase can be reviewed in relation to the original plan and any necessary changes can be introduced into the plan while the project is running. This cycle continues until which point as the entire list of project tasks are completed and the end result meets all of the requirements as defined in the project scope. At this point the project would be considered complete and the project manager can begin the process of closing the project

Revisiting the original project plan throughout the project and seeing if adjustments need to be made during project execution is a good practice because it recognizes that there will be things you don't know at the time you are planning your project, which you will learn when you are working through your project activities. When you have that knowledge, you will want to apply that learning to get closer to your desired project result so you would rework your plan to incorporate what you have learned. That is why they call this process a continuous improvement cycle.

To go even further, the PDCA cycle can be applied to smaller components of your project as well, including groups of activities that are interconnected, as well as individual activities that may have a crucial outcome that must meet a specific requirement to move your project forward. For example, a prize boxer has had a successful career in his weight class and would like to shift to a new weight class. In planning for his prize fight in a new weight class, his weight must fall within the defined weight parameters for the fight on the date of his weigh-in. All planning and execution of his team's project to get the boxer ready for his fight depends on him being the correct weight. This component is vital or else the boxer will not be able to fight at all, and all work that has been done to get him ready would have been wasted effort. Activity by activity application of PDCA would be very difficult to manage and your project team may get the impression that you are micromanaging the project. There is a fine balance that needs to be recognized by the manager and their team, so be thoughtful and give your project the attention it deserves without being overbearing to team members.

So again, our focus will be on walking you through the PDCA cycle with the assumption that you will be initiating either the project or some form or activity prior to entering the cycle, and at the conclusion of the cycle you will either re-plan an aspect of the project to make corrections or to get closer to your defined goal, or will close out of the cycle because you have reached your desired goal. Visually represented, the process you will be following would look like this:

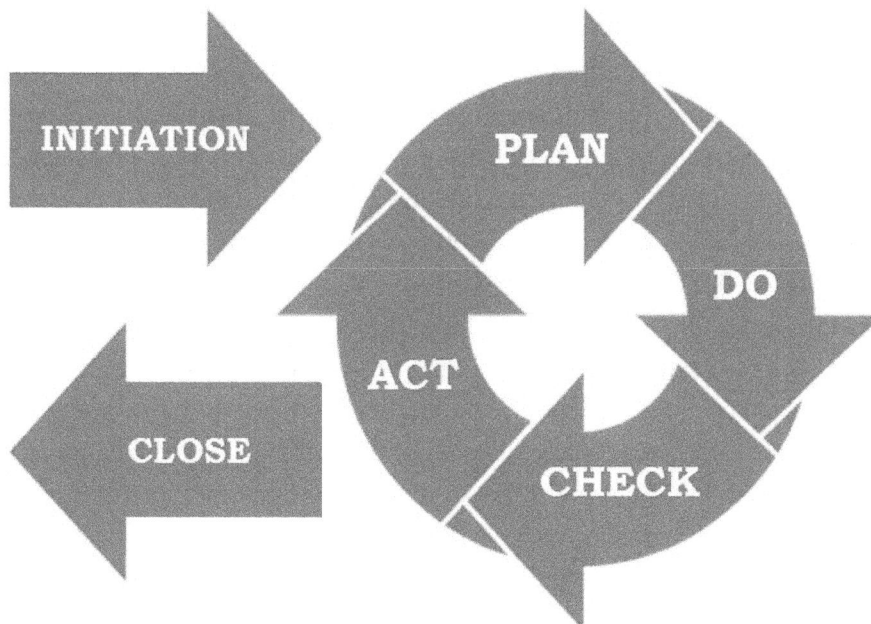

You can see how closely the PDCA cycle matches the IPDCAdC cycle. Now that you have a bit of background on the method you will be using, let's jump right in and get this project started.

Project Planning Workbook

Developing Your Plan

Planning

Once you have defined and documented the goal of your project, (to build something, create something, change something, etc.) you must begin the process of planning. One of the examples I use when coaching executives through the project planning process, especially when mapping where you are now against where you want to be after the project is complete, is to see yourself sitting in front of a large pile of Lego pieces and envisioning what you would like to create. Your project outcome is to build a model from your imagination which you have detailed in your project scope. The Lego pieces represent all the tools, materials, processes, knowledge, and resources you have available to you to build your model. You will break down the defined scope of your model into its component parts, perhaps a base, some arms or legs, a background piece, wheels, or whatever you have envisioned. You will look at the pieces and pick the ones you think you will need to complete each component, group them together, and plan how you will assemble them into your vision. At that point, you would have planned out the work.

To take it one step further toward completing the PDCA cycle and the project as a whole, you could recruit friends or other resources to help you complete your Lego project (your project team). You can describe what you are building by working through your scope with them (onboarding). Then you can assign each person a component to assemble. They would start assembling using the information they have been provided (Execution or DO-ing). You will check their work along the way to ensure they are assembling in the right way and that the end product is what you wanted (Monitoring and Control, or CHECK). You can then either make modifications based on what you or your friend have observed along the way about how the pieces fit together or to get closer to what you have in your mind about the final project outcome (ACT). Once you are happy with each component, your team can try and fit them all together and look at the end product. They may not all fit together properly at first, in which case you may have to make a few changes before you try to build the final model. You would then review your project scope in relation to the final product that has been assembled and see if there are differences between what you have in front of you and what you envisioned would be the end product of the project. If you observe that the model actually built is not exactly what you described in your scope, you would identify what is different and rework your plan to take another pass at getting it right. Of course having gone through the process with your team the first time, you and they will get better at it the second time around. At the end of the second pass, you would perform your check again to see if you are closer to the desired result. You would continue this cycle of planning, doing, checking, and acting/adjusting until either you have met your goal (CLOSE) or you are willing to adjust your scope to match the end product that has been created. In both of these cases, your project would move into the closing process as you exit the PDCA cycle.

Planning is breaking down the goal of a project into its component parts. These parts should be clearly identifiable and manageable for a person or project team to clearly understand. Starting from a goal, each element or aspect of achieving that goal is captured and broken down into its own defined item or task. All of the tasks required to create the project outcome are listed so as to capture everything about the project. In the end, you should be able to look at the complete list of tasks and mentally build the entire project outcome by checking off each item in the task list.

Project planning is the process of documenting project work from start to finish, accounting for as much information in as great a level of detail as possible. Developing a great project plan is the second most important aspect to the success of any project, behind defining a detailed project scope. There is a saying in the world of project management that "projects succeed or fail in planning". This means that good project plans lead to good project outcomes and that poor project plans contribute greatly to project failure. When developing your project plans, think of the largest and/or most important components first and then narrow your focus on the less important components. Start from the big details and then look at the small details. For example, if your project is to build a car, you would not necessarily focus on the color of the car at the onset. Although paint color will be a component of the project, in the planning process, it is a decision that can wait until a later time. You could even just list the item as "Paint Color Decision Required" and schedule that question for a later stage in your project when it is closer to being needed, like after the body has been designed and manufactured. Some project details can be decided later, but there should be a reference in your plan to capture the idea and a time in the schedule to revisit the question. In this sense, smaller less important details can be worked out as the project is rolling as they will not negatively affect the schedule or other more important work.

It is important to break out each task into manageable elements so that it is not overwhelming or difficult to understand when working through each component. For example, if someone told you to build them a house it would be difficult to comprehend, for someone who has never done it before, all the tasks and component parts required to complete the project. If the same person instead asked you to find a supplier of white 100 watt light-bulbs at a cost of under $1.00 each, the task would be clear and easy to understand. Most people can understand the large components of a house construction project such as a roof, doors, windows, walls, lighting, etc. however when you are planning and beginning to execute your project, it is vital to have a complete understanding of everything needed. For someone with no direct experience completing a similar project or a component of a similar project, there are many gray areas where they have no knowledge of the requirements or the tasks involved.

Let's go back to our house building project. For someone who has never done this before, they may have elements of understanding and gaps in knowledge in other areas. In these circumstances, the project manager must document what they know and either research or consult an expert (or someone else that has specific knowledge) to fill in the gaps in their project knowledge. A PM may have a basic understanding that electricity is needed to power lights, appliances, hardwired components of the house, and receptacles for owner use when required. They may not know the building code requirements for wiring a home, the different types and gages of wires needed, the requirement that in wood framed houses wires must be clipped to the framing at specific points, the different types of breakers that would manage different wattage and voltage , the sizes of electrical panels, and the list goes on. In this instance, it is necessary to contact someone who has had direct experience in this component of the project such as a professional electrician.

Consulting an expert is also helpful in the planning stages. Talk to several people who have done what you are looking to do, or at least a component of what you are looking to do, and ask them how they did it, what they used, what steps they took, how long it took them to complete each stage, and what resources they needed to complete the work. Also ask them if there are additional sources of knowledge or resources that might be helpful in furthering your understanding of this work so that you can independently verify the knowledge.

It is important when speaking to people about gray areas of your project that you can actually identify that the person has direct experience or knowledge of the specific area you need clarity on. There are many people who just talk – selling falsehoods and mistruths - seemingly to merely hear their own voice, for the sake of being conversational. If you engage someone with the specific intent of getting information or knowledge you are missing, make sure they are talking from experience. Ask them when was the last time they did this kind of work, what projects they have lead or participated in related to the topic, etc. Probe a bit deeper to make sure the knowledge you are getting is not misinformation.

Going back to our example of the importance of selecting paint color in a project to build a car, how would this project differ if the scenario was slightly changed to represent it as a real world project in the Auto Industry? Let's work through another iteration of the same project, but with a twist. You are a professional project manager working for an Auto Manufacturer, and your project is to build 10,000 gold color cars within 6 months. In our first scenario, a decision about paint color was not as important because we were only building a single custom car and the paint color could be decided at a later time due to the small quantity. In our second scenario, due to the scale of our project, and the time constraints on the project completion, the decisions surrounding paint color need to be worked into the plan at the beginning of the planning process. The project sponsor must decide on a specific shade of gold for the car exterior and the project team would have to source a supplier for the paint, at a price point that is consistent with the budget set aside for the paint. Also, the project team must ensure the supplier delivers the paint at the specific intervals needed during the production of the cars so as not to incur storage costs for housing the paint. Because this scenario is more specific with relation to the paint, due to its importance to the project, more details must be worked out early in the project and additional safeguards must be put into place with the supplier to ensure this component is managed properly. Scoping out the paint component to the level of detail we have above will allow us to create a specific contract with the supplier that details our terms and identifies possible penalties for the supplier's failure to meet the outlined terms. In large projects like these, many key aspects are captured in contracts to lower the risk of specific failure on the part of a supplier or service provider.

Consider the development of your project plan like you are giving a friend directions to get from their house to a meeting place that they have never been to. You might use the usual, turn left here, turn right here method, combined with travel this distance and identify landmarks along the way, all in the hope of capturing the journey well enough so that your friend does not get lost. Your project plan is your map of all the steps you and your project team need to take to get from where you are now to where you need to go to achieve your goal as clearly defined in your scope. Any missing information can be filled in as you go along during the controlling and monitoring phase and additional tasks or directions can be added to keep your team on track.

As you begin working on small goals you will get better and better at breaking down the work needed to achieve your goals, and better at identifying, researching and filling in the gaps in knowledge to provide an increasing level of accuracy in your planning efforts so that you can tackle larger and more complex projects to achieve greater goals. As you begin your journey to apply some of the skills I have outlined above, here are a couple of final thoughts before you dive into the steps in project plan development.

Projects are not run in a vacuum

Projects are never run in isolation, in a static world, or in a vacuum. Projects must be run in a world where there is constant change and a flow of positive and negative events that could possibly impact the successful completion of your project. In a fluid world, project plans must be adapted over time to allow project managers to capture their new position or circumstance, and assess whether their direction needs a course correction to remain on target. Whenever you intend to exert energy toward a goal, especially a personal goal, you must expect that there will always be resistance or forces that try to stop you. Like pushing off the wall in a swimming pool to begin swimming laps or hitting the accelerator of your car from a standstill, there is resistance to your effort. From inertia to movement requires effort to break free from the forces of doing nothing to going somewhere. But this resistance dissipates over time and once you build enough momentum, the scenario changes to make it near impossible to stop you. Your forward motion builds speed and force until you reach your goal. Resistance is something to overcome through sheer persistence, continuous focus, and can be factored into your project plan.

Planning for a future eventuality
Predicting the future based on trends, probability analysis and experience/knowledge

When building the space shuttle, the project team planned for technology to exist in the future to perform needed functions that were essential to the success of the project. The technology did not exist at the time of planning the project but the project team had the foresight to know that this technology would exist at a specific point in the future to allow it to be incorporated into the project design. Basically, they had to plan for a future reality that contained the component, to fill the gaps in their project. PMs however are not fortune tellers and cannot predict the future, however when planning a project, they must look to the future to account for any potential changes that may impact their project, negatively or positively, gauge the potential impact of an event and work it into the plan. After all when you set a timeline for completion of a goal or project, the final date is like a moving target. Aiming at it without looking is a sure recipe for disaster whereas keeping your eye on the target, making course corrections along the way and keeping your aim sharply focused on the goal will greatly increase the success of your project and the attainment of your goal.

When planning a complex or long term project, there are risks and challenges that cannot be foreseen at the onset but that must be planned for as a potential eventuality. Planning for the unknown is never easy, however mapping out and defining the unknown is easier when you engage different people with different experiences in trying to achieve similar project outcomes.

Step-by-Step Planning

Depending on your own experience and the experience or your project team, the steps in planning out a project will have varying degrees of detail. Although when you are first learning about projects and the application of project management techniques to achieve results, it is always better to develop plans with as much detail as possible to guide other resources that may not be as knowledgeable, it is up to you to gage the level of detail you are comfortable with in developing your plans.

The core steps in breaking your scope into a project plan include the following:

1. Defining all activities needed to achieve the project scope into a list.
2. Sequencing and grouping all of the activities into a logical order.
3. Determining how long each activity will take to complete.
4. Exploring how much each activity will cost to complete.
5. Deciding which resource will complete each activity.
6. Developing a schedule with the activity information you have identified.
7. Estimating the total project costs based on each activity cost you identified.
8. Determining how you will manage your resources (your Project Team)
9. Determining how you will communicate with your team and how they will communicate to you.
10. Documenting all of the information you have identified above into a comprehensive project plan.

This process is the same for any size project, whereas the time spent working through these steps will vary greatly depending on the size and complexity of the project. Now let's review each step in this process and look at a simple example of a project plan that demonstrates all of the described elements.

<u>Activity Definition Worksheet</u>

Defining all activities needed to achieve the project scope in a list.

Your Scope Statement defines what you want to achieve and now it is time to identify and break down all the activities needed to reach your project outcome. This breakdown can be done any number of ways, and there is no right or wrong way to do it, however regardless of the method used to break down your goal, the final list of activities should look very similar and have a high level of detail attached. In my personal experience mentoring, training and working with new project managers, a method that works well to gain the appropriate level of activity detail is to identify the larger aspects of the project first and then refine those larger items into smaller activities, forming groups of similar or related activities. Again let us use the example of building a house. Beginning with the larger aspects of the project including the foundation, walls, roof, floors, framing, electrical, plumbing, etc. will help us paint our picture of the needed work to meet our goal. If we began with details about a man-cave with a cool audio-visual system, or a kitchen pantry, it would be difficult to put those individual activities into a perspective relevant to building the remainder of the house. Once you have gone through the process of breaking down a project goal into a list of activities a few times, you will develop a personal method that works for you.

So define as many activities with as much detail as possible into manageable chunks of work (work packages), and group similar and/or related activities together. Identify any gray areas that you know exist but that you have minimal or no knowledge or experience with, and try to define the general idea of the gray space. Talk to people with first-hand experience completing similar projects or project work and ask them if your list of activities related to their experience is complete, and add any detail based on their input. Do the same for any independent research or knowledge you are able to dig up from sources in the know.

Refine your grouped list of activities to the lowest possible denominator that will represent a reasonable amount of time. For example, activities that can be completed with a few keystrokes on a computer or within 5-10 minutes are probably too refined. You can group those activities with other similar activities to extend the minimum activity duration to several hours or days of work. Imagine if you were working on a very large and complex project spanning a year or two and it was planned with activities broken down into time values of 5 minutes. Your entire project plan would have between 105,120 to 210,240 activities listed. Keep in mind the lowest duration for the activities you wish to define and if you want to add additional details, add them as notes attached to your main activity. At the completion of this exercise, you should have a concise yet detailed list of activities or tasks needed to achieve the project goal.

Simple Planning Exercise:

Start with one simple personal goal that you have been thinking about but have not acted on to achieve. Define your goal in a brief and concise manner and make sure it meets the SMART criteria in project definition. After you have defined your SMART goal, take some time to breakdown the goal into its component parts as outlined above, starting with the large components and working toward the smaller ones. Provide as much detail as you like, and review the entire list of components at the end to make sure you have thought of everything you think would need to be completed to achieve your goal. After you are satisfied with your planning list, identify two to three people you know that have personally achieved this goal or something similar to your goal. Reach out to these people and ask them to review your goal and planning list, and have them provide their feedback on the tasks you have identified and the steps you have outlined. Ask if they followed the same steps when they completed their goal. Ask if there is anything missing from the list. Ask if they would give special priority to specific tasks on your list. Remember, this is your chance to consult someone who has actually completed a goal similar to the one you have identified, so ask all the questions you can and document any feedback they provide.

Once you have finished talking to the people you identified, assemble the feedback you have documented and review your original list to see if you would change anything based on their experience. Whether you are looking to lose weight, start your own business, write a book, renovate your home, or complete any other personal project, this process of talking to someone who has completed a similar project can always benefit your planning through real world experience and a different perspective. Ultimately the choice is yours, however taking advantage of real world knowledge is always worth considering.

Activity Sequencing Worksheet

Sequencing all of the activities

Sequencing your activities means putting them into a logical order for completion. You can't paint walls if they have not been put up. You can't eat a steak if the steak has not been cooked.

You cannot sell a product which has not yet been developed. We all have a different view of the order of events, but questioning by using logic will play a part in helping you order activities. Simply ask yourself, what must I do first, and then what comes after that. Your logic will guide you and will lead to an order that works. Grouping related events can also help identify your sequence as you are better able to visualize how a smaller group of events or tasks may interact with each other, than a large list of tasks in a complex project. If you feel comfortable grouping a bunch of related tasks into modules and then sequencing the modules, then you can utilize this method. Just remember that some tasks in your modules may be related to or impact tasks in other areas of your project so keep in mind these connections. Also remember that depending on the resources you are planning to recruit or use, some activities can be worked on at the same time to shorten the time needed to complete your project. Go through your entire list of activities and make sure each item is in the right place.

Activity Duration Worksheet

Determining how long each activity will take to complete

Once you have sequenced your activity list, you will make another pass adding how much time you think each activity will take to complete. Now it is important to understand at this point all of the factors that may impact an activity to determine how long it will take to complete so that you can get a fairly accurate duration value. This is where it is important to talk to people with first-hand experience or special expertise with the activity to help provide you with accurate information. For example, if one activity on your list is to plaster a freshly dry-walled room, you may think the only time you need to account for is that needed for the laborer to complete the plaster work. This is only one component of this task. The plaster itself needs to fully dry before another task, like priming and painting, can begin so the drying time of the plaster must be accounted for in your time estimate. You may also want to add additional time as a buffer, in case there is the potential for a rainstorm at roughly the same time as you have set for the plaster work. High levels of humidity will extend the time needed for plaster to dry, so unless you have a safeguard in place such as a portable heater (which may come with additional costs) to keep the area dry and eliminate the risk of high humidity, you will need to incorporate this time into your activity duration estimate. Again, this is where it is important to talk to people with direct experience that can guide you to the right values and pass along their wisdom about the hidden aspects of each activity.

For tasks on your activity list that involve repetition, consider a time estimation tool taken from the concept of an assembly line. Assembly lines are popular for the completion of repetitive tasks because the workers performing the tasks get better at performing the activity the more they do it. Although they have discovered this performance actually wanes over an extended period of time because workers become bored, and the current practice is to cycle workers to different tasks to break the cycle of boredom, the method of calculating tasks completion is relatively the same. A group of workers are assembled and are asked to perform the needed task several times. They are timed while the task is being completed. At the completion of the sequence, the time for completing the sequence is averaged to account for the number if people and the number of tasks completed within the cycle. This will determine on average how long the task would take to be completed. In a manufacturing setting, this is important information that will help determine the production capacity of the assembly line so that the manufacturer can accurately be able to inform its clients of the time needed to fulfil an order. Let's demonstrate this concept in another way using our previous example of folding laundry. If you had large load of laundry and needed to figure out how long it would take you to fold, you would fold a few pieces and time how long it took you to fold those pieces, and then apply this value to the remaining number of pieces. If it took you on average 10 seconds to fold each piece of clothing, and you had a pile of 300 pieces of clothes to fold, you would determine that you could fold 6 pieces of clothing each minute and then divide your 300 piece total clothes value by 6 to arrive as a value of 50 minutes. It is this time value that you have estimated it will take for you to complete your task of folding your 300 pieces of clothes. This technique is a great way to determine fairly accurately the duration of a repetitive task, and also a good way to conceptualize a method of estimation that you can apply in many different ways to arrive at the length of time needed to complete a task.

Applying these techniques to your activity list will help you have a better understanding of the specific dynamics of your project and at the end of this exercise, you will know the order in which each activity will be completed and how long each activity will take to complete.

<u>Activity Cost Worksheet</u>

Exploring how much each activity will cost to complete

Determining the cost of each activity is also a logical process involving the review of resources that will be doing the actual work to complete the task, assessing the cost of tools, supplies or other support systems needed by the resources, calculating time and costs related to overhead and delay (cost of waiting), and any other costs associated to the completion of an activity. Where material and equipment costs are fairly easy to calculate, the costs of human resources should always be calculated liberally to factor in the different paces at which different resources complete activities.

If you are not sure what an activity would cost, get a quote. When asking a company or resource to quote on the time and cost it will take to complete a task, they typically are able to provide you with the quote at no cost. If they do ask for money to provide you with a quote, move on to the next company that will provided you with the information at no cost. Managers of long and/or complex projects frequently issue Requests for Proposals (RFPs) or Requests for Quotes (RFQs) to a handful of qualified parties to obtain information on the costs of performing certain activities within the constraints set out in the project. The information that is returned by the outside parties will provide valuable input into the project plan, schedule, and budget.

When Professional Project Managers look to engage human resources (workers) to complete project work, they often assess factors that will impact the progress of work. These factors speak to the motivation of the individual worker and this information will help act as a guide in planning other areas of the project. Length of time contracts specify that a set amount of work will be completed according to a schedule, with the entire body of work to be completed at the end of the scheduled contract date. Managing contract workers of this type means the Project Manager needs to follow their progress closely to ensure they are on track. The PM must also ensure that nothing is preventing them from moving at the scheduled pace, or else they may ask for additional money to account for the delay. Salaried workers are consistently available however their motivation is entirely internal to themselves. Getting them to produce on a schedule may differ greatly from completing their other regular duties and they may get frustrated at the constant monitoring of their work. Work Package contracts allow a contract worker to get paid at the time of completion of their work. If their work packages can be completed entirely independently, they are able to work at their own pace to complete and deliver their work package as quickly as possible. This affords the worker the greatest amount of flexibility to work at a rapid pace, and typically gets the work done fast. In contracts like this, the PM should be very careful to ensure no corners have been cut and that the product that is delivered by the worker meets all of the requirements set out in the description of their work. Working fast is great for the worker because they can move on to the next project quickly and make more money, but the PM has to make sure they are getting the highest quality work product from the resource. Understanding how to structure the work arrangement with project resources is important in any project, and when you begin planning your own personal or professional projects, you can also apply the same techniques to ensure you get the most out of your project team. Doing so will create a good working environment and will also contribute greatly to better team cohesion and eventual project success.

Your activity costs will add up to form your overall project budget, so if you have grouped activities within the initial planning process, you will be able to determine the costs associated to each group of related activities, the costs for each individual resource, material and equipment costs, and more. This information will become valuable if your scope changes or if unforeseen events crop up while your project is running.

<u>Project Resource Planning Worksheet</u>

Deciding what resource will complete each activity - Developing your Project Team

At this point, with your activity list in hand, you will review the list to determine who or what resources are available to complete each task. Some tasks will require only people, others will require only tools or machines, and others will require both. Some activities can be completed by yourself, others may require a person you know, and yet others will require you to hire an expert or outside resource. What you are looking for when choosing a resource is a mix of the right person for the job who is capable of delivering the expected result from the activity, who is available when you need the work to be completed, and at a reasonable cost.

Don't think you can do everything yourself and don't assume that you or other people can change. We must all recognize our strengths, weaknesses, and limits. A good project manager looks at each team member as well as themselves and figures out first hand through observation and experience, what they do well at and what they are terrible at. These observations help the PM assign resources to tasks they would do well at, and as a PM, you also have to be honest with yourself and realize that people do not change overnight. If you just learned something new or want to change something that has been done one way to another way, it will take time. For example, if a messy person reads a book about organizational skills, at the end of reading the book, they are not instantly transformed into an organized person. They may start using a few techniques from the book to become a bit more organized in their daily life and disregard the rest, or they may fully embrace the content and begin to change their messy ways, however this will take time to show results and the person may backslide. PMs have to take all this into account when they assign work and they need to keep people motivated and excited about the role they are playing in the project.

An important tip when identifying your ideal project team members is to look at their motivations for participating in the project. Within the workplace, if someone is just looking to get ahead and they believe project work is a route to do this, they may not be the best candidate next to someone who is actually interested in achieving the project outcome. Everyone is motivated by something. When your project work has begun, knowing each team member's individual motivations for participating in your project will help you keep their spirits high, keep them focused on what is important to them, and keep them producing. A person who does not have a strong motivation for participating can get easily disillusioned and become a source of negative energy within your team.

As you identify potential project team members, dig a little deeper than just placing their names next to an activity or a series of activities. In larger more complex projects with a fairly small tight knit project team, I like to create a brief profile of each key team member so that I can know what they are all about at a glance. Like a contact card for a salesperson to use in keeping track of previous conversation details, private family details, birthdates, and side deals they have with a specific client, you can do something similar with your team members. It could be as simple as writing some details on an index card for each member, to as complicated as creating a detailed dossier. It will be different for every project and every team, but it is a great tool to keep track of individual motivations, special information you can use to create a personal connection with each team member (likes, dislikes, family, challenges, etc.), details of specific events, and other details that would help them operate and remain a focused and productive member of your project team. You can also update information on project performance of the individual while the project is running. For example, if one of your resources calls in sick or arrives late consistently, you will want to note that in your documentation. This will become useful if you ever needed to complete another project of a similar nature and are considering the resource for a similar role in your new project.

Individual Resource Planning Worksheet

Resources to a project are to be looked at as time multipliers. One hour of work for a single person compared to 10 people working within the same hour is the equivalent of 10 hours of work within that same one hour timeframe. Crashing the schedule using resource multipliers like this is a commonly used technique in project management, as frequently demonstrated on home renovation television shows such as Extreme Makeover, where a flood of resources come together in a short amount of time to complete a project (the construction of a beautiful new home) in a fraction of the time. Carefully planned and executed, the technique of Crashing the Schedule is a great tool, however it could be disastrous if not planned and implemented properly.

For personal projects with goals of lifting the spirit, good project managers can look for multipliers for the soul that will give them and project resources the moral and spiritual strength to keep going. Charity and other non-profit related events that increase happiness in your life and the life of the team is one example. Team events or something more personal and intimate to keep the team going forward and focused can be effective motivators to keep projects running smoothly.

```
┌─────────────────────────────────────────────────┐
│                                                 │
│      Sample Activity Registry Worksheet         │
│                                                 │
└─────────────────────────────────────────────────┘
```

Identifying and planning project resources should add more support to the reality that your project can be successfully completed according to your plan. This should give you the confidence you need to complete the planning process and move on to executing your project.

```
┌─────────────────────────────────────────────────┐
│                                                 │
│                                                 │
│         Project Scheduling Worksheet            │
│                                                 │
│                                                 │
└─────────────────────────────────────────────────┘
```

Developing a schedule with the activity information you have identified

Formal project scheduling is an art that you will learn over time but the basics are very easy to understand and start applying right away. You are half way there at this point because you have already identified the activities, their duration, the resources that will be performing them, and the sequence in which they will be completed.

In an entirely linear sequential project, your schedule would be already done because you already have the sequence of events and their duration. So let us look at the different activity types as they relate to scheduling.

Sequential Activities – are activities that have to be completed in a specific order after another activity has been completed. The work is dependent on a previous task.

Concurrent Activities – are activities that can be completed at the same time as other activities by different resources. The tasks are independent to other tasks.

Activities that need to start at the same time and activities that need to end at the same time are also factors in scheduling and are easily identified in your activity list. Dependencies like these relate to specific outcomes happening at specific times in order to minimize a potential time delay or prevent resources from just sitting there with no work. As you work your way from simple linear projects to more complex projects with many concurrent activities and dependencies, your experience will guide your scheduling to account for these events.

Just to give you a simple example, the process of making a pizza is sequential. You cannot add the pepperoni slices until the dough has been rolled, the sauce spread and the cheese laid. Current software development projects contain many concurrent activities, as many developers can be writing software code at the same time for different functionality in a modular way so that they can be combined at a later time to form the complete application. So creating a project schedule is placing times and dates to your project activities so that you and your resources know when they need to start working on each activity and how long they should take to complete it and move on to the next activity. The easiest way to begin the process of scheduling your project is to place all of the linear sequential activities in complete order and set aside all activities that can be done concurrent to other activities. The complete linear sequential activity list can then be assigned a start date. When you have selected the start date, you would use each activity duration to schedule the start date of the next, and so on until you have start dates and end dates for every task in sequence, and have identified your project end date as the completion date of your last activity. For the remaining tasks that can be completed concurrent to other activities, you can schedule them at logical times where resources are available to complete the work, keeping in mind any dependencies on other activities in your schedule. You do not want these tasks to cause a delay to others tasks, and if you all your resources are being used, you will want to schedule additional resources to work on these tasks to have them completed in a timely fashion according to your schedule.

Now this is a simple way to view project scheduling, however following this as a start will help you witness the project schedule in action and identify other factors that can affect the schedule. One that I will point out right now is the idea that some tasks do not have to be fully completed to have another task begin, especially when there is a relationship between the tasks. For example, if the activity is described as drywalling an entire house, room by room, and the duration for the activity is set at 8 weeks, as the drywalling work is completed in each room, activities such as plastering, painting, finish carpentry, flooring, and others can begin even though the drywalling activity is still going on in other rooms of the house.

Other factors to consider when designing your project schedule include keeping in mind major holidays, school holidays (for those with kids), key dates in the yearly schedule where kids start and end school, people take vacation, etc. These events will have an impact on your schedule as resources may not be available during these times and work on activities may be delayed, so you must plan for the risk of it impacting your schedule and set aside a time contingency to account for this.

Project Cost Worksheet

Budget Worksheet

Estimating the total project costs based on each activity cost you identified and building a budget.

Budgeting is making sure you have the right amount of money set aside for when you need it. Doing it right means you are prepared and will not delay payments, or worse, run out of money before the project is complete.

You have worked through the process of figuring out how much individual activities will cost in a previous exercise, and you'll remember that by adding up all of the individual activity costs you will arrive at your total project cost. This figure will capture all of the resource costs, equipment and material costs, as well as the costs associated to delays and other factors. Turning this total cost figure into a budget is a matter of reviewing activity costs as they are laid out in your schedule and setting aside the proper amount of money to match the expected expenditures as they appear in the schedule, at set intervals. For example, if the first four weeks of a project have only one resource working on activities and the costs are $1,000.00 per week, then you would expect to spend $4,000.00 over the four week period, and would set aside that money so that it is available to you at the appropriate time. Looking forward to the next 4 week period, if your project has 4 additional resources added at the four week mark at the same pay rate per person, in the period of week 5 to the end of week 8 you would have 5 resources costing the project collectively $5,000.00 per week. This means that over that second 4 week period, your total resource cost is expected to be $20,000.00 and this amount of money should be set aside for distribution in that timeframe.

Resource Management Worksheet

Determining how you will manage and schedule your resources

Managing your project resources involves planning when you will need specific resources in your project and lining them up so that they are available at the right time and remain available for the duration of the assigned work. The resources include any and all resources needed to complete the work, whether it be human resources, materials, equipment, capital, or another.

Defining the timing of needed resources is vital to minimizing the potential for project delays. For example, computer programmers need computers to work on and if the computers have not been bought, the human resources' time is being wasted. Painters need paint, drywallers need drywall, printers need paper, and the list is endless. At this late stage in the planning process, you have already defined all activities, have associated resources to each activity, and have identified them within the context of the schedule, so you will know when each resource will be needed. Your resource plan is your guide to identifying all the resources needed in your project, and your resource schedule will help you line up your resources to be available at the right times. A quick review of the information already contained in your project plan will easily provide this information to you so managing your resources and their schedules will be easy.

The next step is deciding how your resources will be managed during project execution. Small projects with few resources can be managed directly by the Project Manager and can be fairly automated wherein you meet with your team as needed, assign work directly, remain available for any team member to obtain guidance on the fly, and receive completed work packages from your team for review directly. Large complex projects may require additional layers of management to ensure there is tactical support to specialized teams. Team leaders represent one type of field support for projects, as do construction supervisors. Computer software design teams are frequently managed by a lead developer who manages the team day to day and reports back to the project manager at set intervals. Managing your project team will adapt to the size of your project, and when you have many moving parts to account for in your project, you will need help keeping track of all the details. Starting with smaller projects and progressing to larger projects will provide you with the time and experience to develop your sensitivity to the needs of team management as well as your own need for information to feel comfortable in the knowledge your team is operating at an optimal level.

Communication Planning Worksheet

Determining how you will communicate with your team and how they will communicate to you.

A communication plan provides details about the needs of the various audiences that have a stake in the project. It describes how the project manager, project team and other parties will communicate throughout the course of the project. The first step in developing your communication plan is identifying the people you need to communicate with. Once you know this, you can detail what specific types of information, instruction, or other content you need to relay in your communications and the frequency at which you should provide said details. You should also specify the preferred method of communication such as email, voice or face to face. Deciding the regularity of team meetings and which team members are required to be present at said meetings would be decided during this step. Requirements for meetings and regular communication with external companies, contractors or other parties can also be reviewed at this stage but are subject to their approval to become a part of your communication plan.

All resources and people with an interest in the project or its outcome should be involved in your communication effort in some way. It keeps people informed, more willing to share information and promotes an environment of trust and openness. Good communication will also identify risks and problems so that they can be managed sooner with better results.

Make it a priority to be transparent, visible and engaged with your project team so that they will feel motivated to do a great job.

Documenting all of the information you have identified above into a comprehensive project plan.

Assembling all of the components of your project in one place is as simple as printing off the material and placing it into a binder or booklet in the appropriate order. Typically it is assembled in the following order:

1. Project scope and background (brainstorming notes).
2. Project Plan
3. Project Schedule
4. Resource Plan
5. Communication Plan
6. Budget

These are all of the essential plans that you have covered to this point in the planning process. Consider documentation as the drawing of your map. It not only provides you with a reference or starting point, but it is also a living breathing plan which will capture the changes that you make along the way to achieving your goal. At the beginning of your project, this documentation shows all of your planning efforts. During the project execution, you will make changes to this plan based on what happens in real life as the project is going on, as you discover new information, manage problems along the way, manage your resources, hit road blocks, and make course corrections. At the completion of the project, you will be able to look back at all of this documentation and recall exactly what has happened or changed from the start of the project to the end of the project. This information will become an invaluable learning tool for you when planning your next project.

Once you assemble your project materials into a booklet or binder, make sure to put a descriptive name on in and keep it close by during the running of your project so that you can add notes and make changes right away. I like to place every bit of information like communications, RFP details and responses, invoices, progress reports, issues that have popped up, and a detailed diary that highlights unique events into my project binders as I go along so that on reflection I can learn from each unique project experience, allowing me to get better and better at planning and running my projects.

If you are using a computer to document your journey and all of your planning information, make sure you have a dedicated folder for your project and subfolders that you can add information to while maintaining a basic organizational structure. When you start your project and have your plan in place, make sure to add the words "Version 1" or "V1" to the computer file. As you make modifications to this file, keep saving the file as a new version by increasing the version number by one, so that you can keep track of what has changed. You can also create a simple document to keep running notes similar to a project diary to highlight observations and unique information that pops up, so that you can reference this knowledge. Again, at the end of the project, you will have a complete accounting of everything that has changed. You can also use folder structures to keep your project information organized so that if you want to reuse some of the information of one project for another project, you can just copy the files from one folder to another and start making any needed modifications. Using templates to help you work through the many repeatable aspects of planning and managing projects, and keeping these in a folder of their own, will allow you to draw from them as you need.

There are many ways to keep all your project information organized and complete, whether in paper form, electronically, or another form. Developing a personal system of organization that works for you is an essential aspect of managing a project and being a good project manager. Logical organization of forms and templates can be supported with a numbering scheme. Similarly, electronic documents can be given logical filenames and be supported with version numbers when forms and templates are being modified often. Central record keeping can help provide easy access to information and can be shared with your project team for reference and training purposes. And resource specific information can help your project team access instruction and guidance to their specific tasks, roles, and responsibilities. Project documentation and organization is a very personal component of managing your project, just remember that you are part of a team as well.

Risk Planning Worksheet

Identifying and Planning for Risks (Good and Bad)

There is a popular saying in project management that goes "Hope for the best, plan for the worst." This means that every PM is optimistic about their plans once they have been created, but it is important to review them activity by activity with a critical eye after the plan has been completed to determine the worst case scenario for each activity or work package. The magic question when trying to envision risks to your projects is "What if?" This question helps form the basis of exploring different scenarios that could take your project into different directions. What if this happens, or what if that happens, or what could happen if this changes? Creatively exploring all the ways people, events, or environment can positively or negatively impact your project is an essential input to your planning because it takes off the rose colored glasses and lets you clearly see the reality of any situation. Because risk is such a broad and all-encompassing array of potentiality, my suggestion to someone new to project management is to start by focusing on the most probable risks and only focus on high and medium level risks (risks that could impact your project by a more than a 25% impact on your iron triangle). For example, if you hire a single person or resource to complete a project with you, there is a potential for that person or resource to get sick, which would delay your project. Knowing this risk is important so that you can put in place measures that would help keep the project on track if the risk ever became a reality. The probability of this risk is realistic and high as it could potentially halt project work entirely. In a short project, it will have an even higher impact. On longer duration projects, its effect may be less.

Typically there are four strategies for managing project risks, which include: **accepting** the risk and absorbing impact into your project; **avoiding** the risk by planning around it; **mitigate** the risk again through planning to lessen any potential impact to the project; or, **transfer** the risk to a third party such as an outside resource under contract that would protect your project and leave the potential impact on them.

Start assessing risk by looking at events or people that could have a significant impact on your iron triangle and begin identifying high level risks and work your way down to medium and lower level risks. You should not be concerned with every potential risk, rather you want to focus on those highly probably risks. We should all be fearful of the potential for the earth to be hit by a large piece of space debris leading to the end of all life as we know it, but accounting for this probability in your projects is not an effective use of your time.

<u>Contingency Worksheet</u>

Plan any contingencies

Project contingencies should be built into every project because regardless of how experienced a project manager is or how well the project has been planned, there will always be unforeseen events that will impact the project in some way. The longer the duration of the project, the larger the contingency values as there is greater opportunity for more events to occur that will impact the project.

If the magic question to discover if there is a risk to your project is "What if?", then the magic question you need to ask when thinking about contingencies is "What would I do if the risk happens?" A contingency is breathing space that you create in projects to offset potential risks that may affect the iron triangle (Time, Cost, Quality/Performance) or your scope. Variations in these 4 key areas that may come from a risk being realized will impact other areas of your project and each project has unique qualities that must be assessed for the level of risk to the 4 key areas.

- Time – setting aside a specific amount of time in the schedule for a specific task or a group of tasks to account for a potential delay in completing a difficult and complex task is one way to keep your plan working. If the task is completed early then this contingency in your schedule is banked for any other unforeseen risks that may pop up throughout the course of the project. Also, based on the time of year you are working through your projects, you must take into consideration dates that your resources may not be available to work. These dates could include official holidays, religious holidays, vacations, sick days, or dates that relate to children such as the start and end of the school year and popular summer vacation times among parents.
- Cost – depending on the complexity of the project you are working on and the potential for changes within the project over the time scheduled for it, you must assess the potential for increasing costs and set aside a dollar value for this in your project budget. Costs can increase for a number of reasons, from product and resource availability, time of year, fluctuations in shipping costs, time delays that impact resources, or numerous other factors. Many experienced project managers set aside a basic budget contingency value for specific types of projects based on their personal experience running similar projects, however each project really deserves specific attention as the dynamics will change each and every time.
- Quality/Performance – as I have noted earlier in this book, Quality and Performance is a measure of how well your project team is working together to complete tasks according to the schedule and produce the expected work result that will eventually encompass the entire scope of the project. Quality of the work meeting expectations is partially a result of properly defining the expectations during the planning stage of the project. If there is a clear expectation of a piece of work and the resource assigned to the work does not meet the expectation, then there is a problem that requires a contingency. For example, if you

order a piece of needed equipment from an overseas supplier and the equipment that arrives is not the right piece, built to the right specifications, or is delayed in manufacturing, this will negatively impact various aspects of your project, including time and cost. Guaranteeing a quality or performance level is one of the most difficult aspects of completing a project and could happen by lack of clear understanding of what is expected, lack of detail in planning, or poor attention to detail. For complex projects, development of a detailed specification is a vital first step, followed by incorporating the most important aspects of the quality and performance expectations within a legally binding contract with the person or company delivering the specific component. If you are outsourcing any activities to an outside party, it would be a good idea to specify the costs and timeline within the framework of a legally binding contract, so that it is locked in and cannot be easily changed. Any contract should also include a holdback provision for the final payment to ensure the resource actually completes and delivers the final work package to you at the specified time. Failure to do so can give you the opportunity to determine and enforce a penalty for non-performance if needed. A contract can outline exactly what you are looking to receive and can also outline penalties for delays and non-performance that is legally binding to the parties supplying the product or services.

To give you a simple example, if you are managing a one week project to repaint 5 rooms in your home with a group of your friends, there are only 7 days where your project can fall off the rails. If you have taken time off of work to complete the painting and are delayed, then there is an impact to your cost. If a couple of your friends cannot make it to help due to illness or other factors, you may not be able to finish the project within the week timeframe. If it rains heavily in the first few days of painting, the high humidity will cause the paint to dry slower, extending the time needed before applying a second coat, thus pushing your painting schedule back. If the paint color does not look the same as it did on the chit in the paint store, new paint may need to be bought to match the expected colors. These are all reasonable risks in a short project and it is quite clear how they could impact the scope and your iron triangle. Contingencies you may put into place to account for these risks may include:

- Renting a dehumidifier
- Asking more friends than needed to help
- Changing the project scope to only paint 4 rooms instead of 5
- Testing the paint color on the walls using a sample size prior to buying large quantities of paint.

For a small project, the risks and time that could be potentially impacted are small, so the contingencies are also small.

Now imagine the same project on a larger scale, such as you being the owner of a large painting company that just won a contract from your local housing authority to paint 5000 rooms within a one year timeframe. A lot more can go wrong in a year and these risks must be accounted for in your plan through the use of contingencies. I will not go into specific detail here but you can imagine the complexity involved in managing all the workers needed, the supply contract for the delivery of paint at regular intervals, the humidity levels at various times of the year, additional supplies of brushes, painters tape, drop cloths, vacations, sick days, and the list of risks goes on and on.

From your Risk Worksheet, start with the highest level risks and work your way down. List the risk name, probability (high/medium/low), project impact (large/moderate/small), and impact description. After this is complete, assess which area of your project will be impacted by the risk and determine which constraint will be affected (time/cost/quality/scope). Indicate the affected constraint(s) in the Impact Area column, determine the value of the impact (in time, cost, quality, etc.), and list the value in the Value of Impact column. Finally, set your contingency value and type in the last column for each risk. Working through this process forces you to think critically about your project and plan for events that can negatively impact it. At the end of this process, you should feel empowered in the knowledge that come hell or high water, you are doing everything possible to make this project a success.

As your experience increases, you will get better at identifying important aspects of projects that could affect other areas, and will develop your own method of gauging the risk and techniques to offset those risks through the use of contingency values. After all, we must all realize that people perform project work and we are all capable of making mistakes. It is for this reason that we must expect a certain level of error, and work that potential for error into our planning.

Sample Project Plan (Simple) – Grocery Shopping for a Dinner Party

Scope: Shop for groceries for a dinner party I will be hosting this evening in my home for my 6 closest friends and my spouse. I plan to cook an elegant meal including appetizers of canapés and crudité, a main course of braised lamb shanks with roasted potatoes and vegetables, and New York cheesecake for dessert, with matched wine for all who wish. I need to start cooking in 3 hours (6pm) so I need to complete shopping for groceries two and a half hours from now.

1. Defining all activities needed to achieve the project scope in a list.
   - Develop my shopping list, broken down by Food, Drink, and Dessert categories
   - Drive to the grocery store
   - Shop for the Food items on the list
   - Visit the liquor store next to the grocery store
   - Shop for the Drink items on the list
   - Drive to the bakery
   - Shop for the dessert items on the list
   - Drive back home in time to begin prepping for dinner

2. Sequencing all of the activities.
   - This project is linear and simple enough that the list I have written to define the tasks seems to be in a good sequence

3. Determining how long each activity will take to complete.
   - Develop my shopping list, broken down by Food, Drink, and Dessert categories (15 minutes)
   - Drive to the grocery store (15 minutes)
   - Shop for the Food items on the list (30 minutes)
   - Visit the liquor store next to the grocery store (5 Minutes)
   - Shop for the Drink items on the list (10 Minutes)
   - Drive to the bakery (15 minutes)
   - Shop for the dessert items on the list (10 minutes)
   - Drive back home in time to begin prepping for dinner (20 minutes)

4. Figuring out how much each activity will cost to complete.
   - Develop my shopping list, broken down by Food, Drink, and Dessert categories (My time - Free)
   - Drive to the grocery store (My time – Free, $2.00 in gas/insurance/wear and tear on my vehicle)
   - Shop for the Food items on the list (My time – Free, Food Cost $125.00)
   - Visit the liquor store next to the grocery store (My time – Free, Car – None as I'll walk)
   - Shop for the Drink items on the list (My time – Free, Drink Cost $60.00)
   - Drive to the bakery (My time – Free, $2.00 in gas/insurance/wear and tear on my vehicle)
   - Shop for the dessert items on the list (My time – Free, Dessert Cost $20.00)
   - Drive back home in time to begin prepping for dinner (My time – Free, $4.00 in gas/insurance/wear and tear on my vehicle)

5. Deciding what resource will complete each activity. (developing your Project Team)
   - Just myself with the use of my car.

6. Developing a schedule with the activity information you have identified.
   - I would like to begin at 3pm so that I can have a bit of a buffer (1hr) so that I don't have to rush the food prep when I get home. My schedule will look like this:

3:00pm – 3:15pm	- Develop shopping list, broken down by Food, Drink, and Dessert
3:15pm – 3:30pm	- Drive to the grocery store
3:30pm – 4:00pm	- Shop for the Food items on the list
4:00pm – 4:05pm	- Visit the liquor store next to the grocery store

4:05pm – 4:15pm	- Shop for the Drink items on the list
4:15pm – 4:30pm	- Drive to the bakery
4:30pm – 4:40pm	- Shop for the dessert items on the list
4:40pm – 5:00pm	- Drive back home in time to begin prepping for dinner

7. Estimating the total project costs based on each activity cost you identified.

Total Costs:

My time –	None
Gas/Insurance/Wear and Tear of Vehicle -	$8.00
Food Costs -	$125.00
Drink Costs -	$60.00
Dessert Costs -	$20.00

Total Costs: $213.00 (your dinner party budget)

8. Determining how you will manage your resources (your Project Team)
   - The only two resources in this project are myself and my vehicle, so I will manage them both directly.

9. Determining how you will communicate with your team and how they will communicate to you.
   - Since I will be completing all the tasks myself in this exercise, I will not need to communicate with anyone, however I will keep track of my results as the project is running so that I can learn for the next time I plan to throw a dinner party.

10. Documenting all of the information you have identified above into a comprehensive project plan.
   - A formal documented project plan may look like the following template, but you can totally customize your plan to a form which you are comfortable with and that you can logically follow, so long as the components within your plan consist of all the required elements.

Grocery Shopping for a Dinner Party – Project Plan

Scope: Shop for groceries for a dinner party I will be hosting this evening in my home for my 6 closest friends and my spouse. I plan to cook an elegant meal including appetizers of frozen canapés and crudité, a main course of braised lamb shanks with roasted potatoes and vegetables, and New York cheesecake for dessert, with matched wine for all who wish. I need to start cooking in 3 hours (6pm) so I need to complete shopping for groceries in two and a half hours from now.

Schedule (3pm Start)	Tasks (Activities)	Duration (Minutes)	Cost (Dollars)	Resources
3:00pm – 3:15pm	Develop my shopping list, broken down by Food, Drink, and Dessert categories	15	$0.00	Me
3:15pm – 3:30pm	Drive to the grocery store	15	$2.00	Me, Car
3:30pm – 4:00pm	Shop for the Food items on the list	30	$125.00	Me
4:00pm – 4:05pm	Visit the liquor store next to the grocery store	5	$0.00	Me
4:05pm – 4:15pm	Shop for the Drink items on the list	10	$60.00	Me
4:15pm – 4:30pm	Drive to the bakery	15	$2.00	Me, Car
4:30pm – 4:40pm	Shop for the dessert items on the list	10	$20.00	Me
4:40pm – 5:00pm	Drive back home in time to begin prepping for dinner	20	$4.00	Me, Car

	Total Time	**120 Minutes**	
	Total Cost		**$213.00**
Number of People **8**	**Cost Per Person**	**$213 / 8**	**$26.63**

Resource Management   **Direct**
Communication   **Direct**

This is a project that is easy to understand, simple to follow, contains all of the information needed to see it all the way through and provides all of the details required to capture the elements of Time, Cost, and Scope/Quality. Now let's begin tinkering with this plan to see how things would change if a few elements are redefined or a few curve balls are thrown in.

How would the project change if:

Two guests asked you if they could each bring a friend. (Change in Project Scope)

- The activity list, resources, communication, and schedule would stay the same, because you would still visit the same places and buy the same things, just more of them.

- The cost would increase to account for the two additional people. Since we have broken down the per person costs, we can easily calculate that the cost of adding 2 people would be 2 x $26.63 = $53.26.

You got into your car only to find that the tank was virtually empty. (Unforeseen Risk)

- You would have to add an activity to account for this unforeseen event (or Risk), to visit the gas station to refill your gas tank for the grocery trip, to the activity list and sequence it where it belongs, as the very first item.
- You would have to add the time needed for the new activity (trip to the gas station) to the schedule.
- You would have to re-sequence all of the other items in the list and rework the schedule.
- You would need to add the cost of gas/insurance/maintenance to the new activity.
- You would need to recalculate the overall time based on the revised schedule.
- You will need to recalculate the overall costs and the per person costs based on the unforeseen cost.
- All other aspects of your project would remain the same.

A visiting friend offered to come along and help you shop for groceries. (Additional Resource)

- Your activity list would remain the same, as would the costs (if they are not being added to the dinner party as a new guest).
- Your activity duration will shorten for any item where your friend would be able to help concurrent to your activities. The additional set of hands may cut your Food shopping time in half to 15 minutes. If the friend visited the liquor store to pick-up the Drinks while you were completing the Food shopping, the two activities would be acted on at the same time, eliminating the time for the shortest change in duration.
- You would need to think about how you will manage the additional resource.
- You will also need to determine how you will communicate with one another if you are in two different places. (possibly by cellular phone)

You were running this project as part of your catering business and the event was a party for 100 people at a venue which they have paid for. You would only have to provide the Food, Drink and Dessert to the venue staff for their team to prepare for the event. Your modified project plan might look like this:

Grocery Shopping for 100 Person Event at XYZ Venue – Project Plan

Scope: Shop for groceries for an event that you will be managing through your catering company. The event will be a dinner for 100 guests at XYZ venue. The venue staff will prepare and serve all of the food, however we will need to shop for all of the Food, Drink and Desserts for the event, using the same menu as the previous smaller format dinner party, an elegant meal including appetizers of canapés and crudité, a main course of braised lamb shanks with roasted potatoes and vegetables, and New York cheesecake for dessert, with matched wine for all who wish. I need to deliver the food to the venue no later than 6pm on the date of the event two days from today.

Schedule	Tasks (Activities)	Duration (Minutes)	Cost (Dollars)	Resources
3:00pm – 3:45pm	Develop my shopping list, broken down by Food, Drink, and Dessert categories	45	$0.00	Me
3:45pm – 4:00pm	Drive to the grocery store	15	$4.00	Me, Car1 Mary, Car2
4:00pm – 5:30pm	Shop for the Food items on the list	90	$1,562.50	Me, Mary
	Me and Mary Total	**150**		
4:45pm – 5:00pm	Drive to liquor store next to the grocery store	15	$2.00	Sally, Car3
5:00pm – 5:30pm	Shop for the Drink items on the list	30	$750.00	Sally
	Sally Total Duration	**45**		
4:45pm – 5:00pm	Drive to the bakery	15	$2.00	Harry, Car4
5:00pm – 5:30pm	Shop for the dessert items on the list	30	$250.00	Harry
	Harry Total Duration	**45**		
5:30pm – 5:50pm	Drive to venue to deliver groceries for 100 guest dinner. (Me, Mary, Sally, Harry)	20	$12.00	Me, Car1 Mary, Car2 Sally, Car3 Harry, Car4
	Longest Time	**170 Minutes**	The longest Activity set time will represent the ideal time schedule.	
	Total Cost		**$2,582.50**	
Number of Guests	100	**Cost Per Person**	$2,582.50 / 100	**$25.83**

Resource Management
- **Resources would be assigned to tasks**
  - **People – Me, Mary, Sally, Harry & 4 vehicles**
- **Each resource will get a copy of the schedule**
- **Each resource will be supplied with a phone list of all other resources in case of questions or emergencies**

Communication
- **Cellular Phones**
- **Group call 30 minutes prior to the shopping trip to give details**

- In this case, I would start by removing the schedule details and adjust the activity durations to determine when I would need to start shopping for groceries on the day of the event. I have used a factor of 3 to adjust the key shopping times.
- Adjust the costs by dividing each shopping cost by 8 (the original number of guests) and then multiplying the result by 100 to account for the new number of guests.
- Total the additional resources and costs for the additional vehicles.
- Adjust the total project cost and cost per person (which will change slightly due to the additional resources).
- Mary, Sally and Harry's salaries must be worked into the final figures; however we have not done that in this case, assuming it will work through in the final contract with the venue or catering client.
- Note that this project is setup a bit differently as there are 3 additional resources. These resources are all managing one shopping trip. Mary and I are managing the Food Shopping trip. Sally is managing the Drink shopping trip, and Harry is managing the Dessert shopping trip. Because all three trips are being managed separately, the times for each trip will overlap as they are being completed concurrently (at the same time) and not sequentially (in order, one after another). When redesigning the schedule, I have taken this into account so that the start time of each trip is adjusted. The total time of the schedule in this case will become the longest trip (the Food shopping trip), so this activity will start before all of the others.
- The new project schedule will begin at 3pm and will end at 5:50pm; however the resources will not have the same number of hours worked. Mary will be working 2 hours and 50 minutes whereas Sally and Harry will be working only 1 hour and 5 minutes each.
- In this reworked schedule, take note that there is only a ten minute buffer. Should any unforeseen events pop up during this project, this may not be enough time to salvage an on-time delivery.
- There is also the potential for a volume discount when shopping in large quantities, so this may be positive risk that may represent a lower overall project cost.

As you can see from these four examples, making small or large changes to a project will affect other areas of the project. Some minor changes may be easily managed with minimal adjustments, while large changes may require a total rework of the project plan. This is a clear demonstration of how the Iron Triangle works with the project constraints of Time, Cost and Scope/Quality to show some of the ways in which interactions between these key elements may filter down and represent changes within a project.

Executing Your Plan

Do

At this point, you have defined your Scope Statement in detail and have created an amazing project plan. You can imagine how the project will run from this point until a successful conclusion and you should be getting more and more excited. Already you have taken many more steps than the average person would to achieve their goals and dreams. From this point forward, the momentum you have been gaining along the way will help you steam roll over any problem or hurdle you may encounter and your creativity and excellent planning will keep you on course. Now the fun part begins ... executing your plan!

Executing the first steps of your plan with your team

Doing the work as detailed in your plan starts with a process called on-boarding, which simply put means talking to the resources you have identified, explaining the project and the role you will be asking them to play in completing the tasks you have assigned. Your project plan has identified all of the activities within your project and the resources you have assigned to complete each activity. Providing your resources with information about the tasks you have assigned to them and making sure they understand the expected outcome from each task is important. Depending on the type of project you are working on, personal, business, work related, or another type, the resources could have different levels of commitment. If you are paying for the resource, you should have their full commitment. If you are not paying the resource, then you need to have a backup plan to complete the activities in case the resource cannot fully complete the work you have assigned. Giving your team members a breakdown of each assigned task and the outcome is like giving them a scope for each task. This is what you are looking to achieve, this is how it will be achieved, and this is exactly what you are looking for at the end of each activity.

Making sure your team understands what you are looking for is vital, but this process is not just you providing them with instructions. It is a dialogue that you are having with your team members so that you can determine if they have the skills and knowledge needed and are fully capable of actually delivering what you are looking for. There should be a candid discussion about their comfort level and their ability to complete the tasks you are assigning to them according to the schedule you have developed. If there are knowledge gaps or foreseeable difficulties with the schedule, they should be identified at this stage and your plan adjusted to fill those gaps or adjust the schedule. Also, you should convey that this is a team effort and that you will be available to help facilitate and support them in the performance of their activities.

Lining up resources

Once your team members have committed their involvement to the project, you can run through your project plan and confirm you have all of your human resources committed to the work they have been assigned. Next you would look to line up all of the resources that are non-human, including any equipment, materials, outside products or services, and any other resources you have identified in your plan. If a portion of your project involves an outside company or contract worker performing tasks or supplying a solution, then you would begin the process of engaging them so that they can commit to the schedule and outcomes you have identified for them. Remember, it is a good idea to capture as much detail in the form of a legally binding contract with any outside parties. It could be as simple as writing the details of work and your expectations on their quote and then having them or a company owner sign and return a copy to you. For product orders, make sure the specific target dates are listed in the agreement and any specific product details of particular importance appear on the invoice or in some documented form that you can refer back to if there is a problem. As I mentioned earlier, if you are outsourcing any activities to an outside party, it would be a good idea to specify the costs and timeline within the framework of a legally binding contract, so that it is locked in and cannot be easily changed. Any contract should also include a holdback provision for the final payment to ensure the resource actually completes and delivers the final work package to you at the specified time. Failure to do so can give you the opportunity to determine and enforce a penalty for non-performance if needed. Following this practice when dealing with outside resources helps you manage project risk and ensures you get exactly what was agreed to in your defined contract scope.

At the end of this process, all of your resources, both human and non-human should be lined up, are aware of what work they will be doing and when they will be doing it, and know what the expected outcomes are for their activities.

Assemble your team – Kickoff Meeting

Formally kicking off your project is a good way to build enthusiasm and promote good group relations within a project team. Having insight into individual project tasks may not give your team a full understanding of the project as a whole, and this meeting is for you to outline the project scope and give your team confidence that they will be a part of something great, something that has been planned from start to end, and something that can truly be achieved if everyone plays their part well. Remember, nobody can accomplish greatness alone. They always have some form of support system.

Having met with each team member individually at this point, now it's time to get your entire project team together as a group. This could be a face to face meeting, a conference call, or a bit of both. Whatever works so that as many people involved in the project are all together and can participate.

The meeting does not have to be a long drawn out affair. All you need to do is welcome the members, introduce them to one another, explain the scope of the project, and why this particular team is ideally suited to deliver a successful outcome to the project. You may also want to give your team an opportunity to mingle amongst themselves and make specific introductions with members that will be working closely together. I like to frame it like an office birthday meeting promoting light social interaction between members, and some coffee and a cake is always a good idea.

You can conclude the meeting casually, letting members know that you will be in touch shortly to provide more specific individual details and get the project moving to begin on the set start date.

Assigning work to your team

If you have assembled your project plan using the templates that I have provided, then you will have a resource by resource breakdown of project work. You have already met with each team member and gaged whether each has the specific skills and knowledge required to complete the activities they have been assigned in your project plan. You have also introduced them to the rest of the project team and filled them in on the scope of the project. At this point you are ready to review with your team the individual activities you have assigned to each member. This can be done in a group wherein you work through the entire project plan and each resource in their scheduled order, or you can meet one on one with each member and then each working group to give more personal attention and level of importance to each member. Whatever ways you are comfortable passing this information down to each team member, follow your instinct.

Once you have completed giving all team members their activity lists and explaining the content and expectations, you are almost ready to begin your project.

Setting aside money

As I discussed previously, your project budget is the total costs you have identified being released according to your project schedule. You have gone through mapping the money needed at each stage of your schedule. Now it is time to take your full project budget and ensure that each stage has its budget ready for release. The last thing you want is to delay the project because you have run out of money or have experienced cash-flow problems that will delay the payment of resources.

Whichever way you feel comfortable segmenting your weekly, monthly, stage, or other payment schedule to set aside funds, document the needs of the time period you set and ensure the actual money is earmarked and set aside for the specific dates as needed. This could mean using two bank accounts, one for holding funds to be released and one to hold the remaining project budget, as well as a series of reminders or calendar notices indicating the funds that need to be present at each stage of the project. Developing a system that keeps you aware and prompts action to ensure the correct amounts are present at key times is specific to you and your management system and style. Just make sure you document the system you are using to manage the budget so that you can review it later and make modifications as needed.

Kicking off your project

After all of your introspection, reflection, research, planning, scheduling, documenting, budgeting, networking, and other efforts, the day is finally here. The start date of your project will be filled with anticipation, excitement, and most likely a hint of fear ... which will pass quickly once you look at the body of work that you have built to support the future success of the project. This transition from planning to doing is really just a very small event in the complete picture of the project, but it should really be savored for all the hard work that has built up to that moment. Like a sports coach that has trained and guided his team to the final match in a championship, you hope that you have given them enough knowledge and have pushed them hard enough to perform well with minimal coaching to achieve the big prize.

Managing resources

Your team is ready and you have released them onto your project with a ferocity and drive to succeed. What you will realize quickly is that there may be slight to severe frustration with some team members. Part of your job from here on in is to balance being there to help when they need it and stay out of their way when they don't. Managing your resources is keeping aware of where they are in your schedule, what tasks they are working on, and that they are where they should be. Part of your role as PM is to make sure resources are working well together, so getting involved in the groups and actively promoting good communication and relations is very important.

Remember that the structure and pace of project work is different than that of normal day to day operational work. You need to keep in mind that most people are used to working in a regular work environment where there may be deadlines but where the pace of the job is fairly steady and allows for an even relaxed execution of their work. Project work is entirely different in this respect as the pace by comparison is extremely fast, the emphasis on frequent, detailed and specific communication is of particular importance, and the impact of an individual problem may impact many other people. Because you are trying to accomplish something unique and wonderful at an accelerated pace, there is extra emphasis on reporting, feedback, progress monitoring of tasks and follow-up because there are many more interdependencies within project work that may adversely affect multiple areas of the project as a whole. Although some people may be challenged to adjust, your job as a PM is to help facilitate and transition their way of thinking to a project team approach. Working with a focused team to accomplish something that has never been done before is a valuable experience but it does have its challenges. This shift from one extreme to another will highlight the distinction between the regular work pace and the project work pace.

When you do see that a project team member is having challenges adjusting, step in to support them before they start to slide. Help the team member reflect back on what motivated them to get involved in the project. If their motivations have changed, work with them to include them in the project in a way that they are comfortable with moving forward. Help your team members understand your perspective on the project and highlight the importance of their contribution to the success of the project. Speaking openly and honestly can be difficult but is vital especially to project work because the success and effectiveness of your team to work together drives overall project success.

Monitoring progress

Progress in a project is easily seen by observing the completion of activities or work packages. When activities are completed by a resource, you would check what has been produced by each activity to ensure in meets the defined specification for that end product. For example, in the process of building a car, one project team may be tasked with designing a headlight array. A specification would be drawn up prior to starting that project groups' work, to provide details about the electrical inputs to the lamp array and from the body designers to give information on the mounts and dimensions of the openings for installing the lights. After the headlight design group has told the PM that their tasks are complete, the PM would check their work against the specifications set out by the electrical and body teams to ensure all the components will fit together as expected. If there is a discrepancy, the PM would go back to the headlight group and ask them to make corrections. Keeping the team on track, making sure they are in the correct spot according to the schedule, and making sure the work they are delivering is what is expected is all part of monitoring progress. This is where collecting data on what was expected and what was actually delivered by the resource completing the project work is important as it will feed into the next phase of the cycle.

Follow your project schedule and label tasks as completed as soon as they are delivered to specification. You can use color coding or another labelling system to indicate completed tasks. Any areas that are not producing results according to the schedule should be highlighted as areas of potential concern, and you should spend a bit more time with the team members having difficulty to pull them through the schedule to where they need to be. The important thing to remember here is the difference between regular work and project work. As I mentioned earlier, project work is completed at an accelerated pace compared to regular work, and because this is the case, a small delay, problem, or project slippage can become a big problem very quickly. Monitoring progress in this environment means making quick and accurate assessments whether the activity outcomes meet the planned outcomes, communicating much more frequently with your project team, and stepping in to provide guidance and solve problems earlier … before they become BIG problems.

<u>Problem Management Worksheet</u>

Managing problems

Problems will crop up in every project, and typically at the worst times. Staying aware and informed about the progress of your project, and communicating openly and honestly with the project team will help create a healthy environment to managing any problems. When something does crop up, there are a few steps you can take to work through each problem to effectively address it.

1. Define the problem in detail – capture the problem details as closely as possible.
2. Identify the affected activities in your project – highlight affected activities in your project plan, accounting for who or what is impacted, any additional costs to the budget or timeline, or affects to the quality of an activity outcome or the project outcome as a whole.
3. Determine the current and potential impact on other interdependent activities in the project – rate the severity of the problem now and how severely it would impact the project later on if it is not dealt with immediately. This should provide you with a timeframe for your actions to address the problem.
4. Decide what to do to deal with the problem
   a. Ignore it – people sometimes see problems where there are none and many minor problems have a way of working themselves out with no action required whatsoever. If you have determined that there would be minimal to no impact on any parts of the project, then you can ignore it.
   b. Absorb it by recognizing it and taking no action – absorbing a problem stems from first determining the impact and then checking if you have enough of a contingency built into your project to easily account for this impact. If so, you are able to absorb the impact of the problem and keep moving forward. Just be careful that the problem is fully dealt with and does not fester and grow.
   c. Mitigate it – mitigation is putting in place a solution that lessens the impact of a problem. Like insurance, it limits your exposure to a negative outcome. Having a back-up supplier for a key supplier is one example of this. The secondary supplier may cost a bit more for the same product, but having their information available would help you in the event the primary supplier cannot deliver their product on time. Every key component in your projects should have a back-up plan in the event of slippage.
   d. Avoid it by taking steps to deal with it – some problems can be predicted in advance, and when they are, you have the option of taking steps to put in place a solution that eliminates the problem entirely. Purchasing different currency to pay an overseas supplier in advance of their product delivery is one example of avoiding the problem of unforeseen currency fluctuations.

e. Reduce the impact of it by taking an alternate approach – re-planning a component of your project to deal with a problem is quite common practice, especially if the potential impact to the project it high. Exploring alternate approaches that would maintain your Iron Triangle with minimal impact, involves working with your project team to get creative and think outside of the box.

f. Transfer it to someone else – this can involve bringing in an expert or buying a solution that totally offloads the problem onto the shoulders of someone else. You many need to spend a bit of additional money to get this done but if the cost is worth it in the long run by eliminating costly overruns or resource delays, then you are ahead of the game by transferring it to a third party.

g. Handle it through a combination of the above – again, project management is about building and creating something new, so dealing with problems will let you get better at finding creative solutions to complex problems.

5. Check your Iron Triangle to see if you need to make any adjustments – having defined the problem, determined its full impact on areas of your project, and come up with ways to manage it, you are now able to look at the potential impact to your iron triangle (time, cost, quality/performance). Typically there is a clear impression of at least one area that would be affected by the problem directly. Once this area is identified, you would simply need to factor in the effect on the other two sides of the triangle to ensure your plan is adjusted properly to reflect where you are now and what things will look like when the problem has been addressed. You may need to adjust your timeline, your budget, or the level of quality of your end product, but you are more intimately aware at this point about the details of your project and are most capable of choosing the priorities to focus on preserving.

Managing problems is a special skill that can only be gained through real world experience. When they do arise, capture the information and make your decisions based on real data and information present. Do not engage your emotions and do not make it personal. If you are working on a personal development project, although it may be challenging to separate yourself from being emotionally involved, remember that you have a goal to achieve and reaffirming your commitment to achieving your goal will help drive you through the lows to even greater highs. Remember, a problem is a "temporary" road block that allows a good PM to flex their creative muscles and demonstrate leadership to the team. Nothing builds loyalty quicker than helping a team member work through a problem and demonstrating that you have their back without blaming them.

Finally, throughout the process of executing the work you have planned, you will come across valuable information and knowledge you did not have when you initially planned the project. This new knowledge should be documented or otherwise captured in some way so that it can be referenced at a later time. There are a variety of lessons to be learned when working on projects, from project specific details related to technical aspects, to procedural and process knowledge, from how your team interacts with one another, your own management skills and approach to the team and individual members, and even the performance of outside parties. Although the term coined for this is lessons learned, you can consider this part of your learning process for becoming a better project manager, and embracing this knowledge is what makes it possible for you to grow and develop toward tackling bigger and better dreams and goals in the future.

The execution of your project plan, or the "DO-ing" of the work, represents the fruit of many hours of your effort in thinking about and planning to achieve your goal, choosing the right team, bringing them up to speed, finding the budget to see your project through to its successful conclusion. Watching the first tasks of your project being executed and delivering results should really be a positive moment for you as an affirmation that this is really happening, that your goal will be achieved and that you are doing what most people will never do ... reach for their dreams and really take an honest shot at achieving them. Every project manager has a different personal management style and will focus on different things when working with their teams. What I would stress from personal experience would be for you to focus on your project plan, your schedule, and tasks that your team is currently working on to ensure they are being completed with the results you had in mind. Checking in on your team and making them aware that the lines of communication are always open is another positive practice which promotes your approachability and lets your team feel comfortable bringing up issues that might well have festered otherwise. It is important to remember that doing the work is actually work. Yes, it is exciting being part of a team and the collegial environment is new to many people, but the goal is to produce work at the defined pace and in the right order to keep everything moving forward smoothly. Review your project plan, or at least the week or two that you are currently working through daily and take the pulse of the team regularly.

Eyes Wide Open – Monitoring Progress and Results

Check

The process of checking the product outcomes of each activity is part of your continuous monitoring throughout project execution. As your team starts producing results, you check those results against what you have planned to see if there is a match. Monitoring performance is done in the moment throughout the entire execution process and works hand in hand with the work being completed. After all project activities have been completed, a big picture review or CHECK can be done.

Checking Progress Against Project Scope

Your team has completed work on the activities they have been assigned. These are called the actual results. Now it is time to check them against what you were hoping the activity would produce, when you initially documented the activity on your project plan, or planned result.

When comparing the planned result with the actual result, take note of any differences between the two, and also take note of any additional information that has emerged during the execution of the work that was not available during the planning process that would have been useful. This process also reviews the actual doing of the work by your project team as well as how you managed the team through the execution stage of the project.

Quality/Performance Check

Is everyone doing their work, at the pace you expected, according to the timeline you initially laid out? Are your resources being used up at the pace you expected, quicker or slower, do you need to adjust the schedule or cost? Do you need to dip into your contingency? Checking the quality of not only the products that are being created as a result of the project activities, but the way they are being produced by your team and how the team is interacting together as a unit is vital information needed by the project manager. After all, you are managing your team to produce results and they need to be as effective and efficient as possible in the completion of their work to have your project succeed. Minor to major variances in the performance of team members and the outcomes they produce can have a major impact on the project as a whole, so take the time to assess how your team is working together and ensure you clear a path to good relations and a good work environment.

Team Meetings

Meeting regularly either informally or formally, as a full project team or even smaller groups keeps the lines of communication open, promotes trust, and allows you to remain aware not only of project successes but challenges that team members may be having. You will not necessarily be seeing all of the moving parts of your project working at the same time, so communicating with your team will allow their observations to be shared and incorporated into your lessons learned. Brainstorming as a group while the project is running gets everyone on the same page, makes them aware of the overall project progress, and allows their input and observations to have a positive impact.

Identifying and Removing Roadblocks

Through your team meetings and/or communicating directly with team members, you will become aware of current or potential roadblocks that could pose unforeseen problems to your project. Remember that some team members might have a "don't shoot the messenger" mentality which may prevent or delay the presentation of valuable information about a problem. Keeping the lines of communication open, remaining on top of your project and being aware of where team members are in their individual activities, promoting an environment of trust, and keeping a close eye on the project schedule to catch any slippage, are all important aspects of identifying a real or potential roadblock. One you recognize that a roadblock or problem exists, work with your project team or specific team members to categorize it, assess the severity of it, and develop solutions to deal with it.

Jeepers Creepers

Throughout the process of working on your project activities, producing work outcomes, and reviewing actual project results, you and your team will develop insights and observations about the viability of your project scope. These insights and observations are a reality check that can be used to re-assess your project scope. This is not designed to totally redesign your project scope, only to add a dimension that was impossible to see during the isolated planning process. Adding new components to the project, new features, elements that were not originally thought of, will run through your mind at this stage, as most project managers want to produce a fantastic product that is bigger and better that anyone has seen before. It is important take hold of those emotions and channel them into preserving the project scope and making only minimal yet essential modifications. The term "scope creep" refers to an ever increasing scope while the project is being executed, with additions being tacked on, changes being made, and rework being planned and performed. It is easy for this to get out of hand, so make sure you are aware of the pressure to modify your scope and manage it appropriately.

One way of managing scope creep is to keep track of all changes and additions brought up during the execution of the project, and assemble them into a separate project to be completed after the original scope of the project is met. This would allow the time and costs of the additional work to be assessed independently without interfering with the original project work. If it can be done after the original project work is completed, then it should be looked at as a micro-project to be scoped separately, provided with a timeline and assigned to a resource after the main project is complete Another approach to take if the changes or additions are needed within the original project timeframe, would be assigning the changes or additions to a new resource. Having a new resource manage changes and additions will allow your original project team to remain focused on their current work and minimizes the amount of time and effort it will take you and the team to try and integrate the changes, cost out the changes, and implement the changes into the existing schedule. From experience, minor changes can easily turn into major changes to project scope, so tackle minor changes if they can be incorporated within the original project scope, but anything that would push the existing definitions set out in your iron triangle should be managed as a micro-project, to be scoped separately, provided with its own timeline, and assigned to new resources after the main project is complete.

Adjusting Your Plan

Act (Adjust)

Taking action at the end of the PDCA cycle is a decision making step that involves taking all of the experience and knowledge you have gained from the first pass through your project plan, or whatever smaller increment of measurement you are using in the application of the cycle, to choose a course forward. If based on your observations, you have met all of your project objectives, you have paved the way to begin closing out your project. If there are new developments or deficiencies in your project that needs to be addressed, then this is the stage in which you would begin the process of re-planning your project to correct the outstanding issues. Finally, if your project has stalled or has hit a major roadblock that you have assessed to be insurmountable at this point in time, then it is at this point where you would decide to abandon, shelve, or kill your project. Simply stated, this part of the cycle is a decision making point based on observation of the current state of the project. It also allows you an opportunity to capture information that will be useful if the decision is made to continue with the project with an altered plan or project scope.

Your options at this stage may include:

- Accept (or Adopt) – involves accepting the result of the project work as meeting or being a close enough match to your original scope to consider the project objective met, and to begin closing your project.
- Adapt – means taking all of the information available to this point, including your own observations, team member observations, and project work results, and incorporating any changes or adjustments to your project scope, and incorporating them into the process of re-planning your project for the next pass.
- Abandon – is a word you hope to never hear as a Project Manager, but it is an unfortunate reality of some projects. There could be a variety of factors that lead a project to be abandoned, from difficult environments, failure of the project team to produce results, external challenges and pressures that could not be avoided, competition from another party to complete the same goals, or other events and circumstances that have contributed to poor results. One historic example of this is the race to the moon between the USA and Russia. Once the Apollo astronauts touched down on the surface of the moon, the Russia project with the same scope had failed. The premise of both projects was to be the first to achieve a lunar landing, and since only one of the parties could be first, the successful landing would have ended the project for the other. Although projects fail from time to time, there is a wealth of knowledge and information that can and should be gathered and documented for future use. Not only can you learn a lot from a failed project, but there are instances where projects have been revived and executed under different circumstances and at different moments in time to achieve astonishing successes because the landscape had changed to create a more favorable environment.

How is your team doing – Keeping them motivated

At this decision making point, it is a good idea to assess the general motivation level of your team. Remaining cohesive and involved at this point is important especially if you decide to initiate another pass at the PDCA cycle in order to make adjustments, correct issues or re-scope a portion of the project. Rework is never fun but getting the project right is the overall goal. Keep your team involved in the process, communicate and listen to their thoughts and observations, and validate their perspectives all while remaining focused on completing your project well.

Capturing any needed changes

From your last pass through the Check process, you should have defined any deficiencies, modifications, and scope adjustment you and your team were able to observe. Now is the time to decide which of the items in your list will be ignored and which will pass through to the next stage of re-planning. As the project manager, your focus is on achieving the scope of the project, and while there may be opportunities to create something really exceptional, that decision will impact many factors.

The limiting properties of a project format are both a positive and negative trait. It is positive because it defines a set of parameters that impose a reality onto the framework of the project design taking into account real world limitations such as limited funds, time constraints, and scarce resources. It is negative in a sense that there are things you will see within the management of a project that can be made really exceptional if pursued. These potential earth-shattering breakthroughs are limited by the constraints of the project, but the insight you gain into them should be well documented so that they will not be lost and can be revisited when the time is right.

So refine your list of changes and additions and make your selection on what if anything will be in your next pass through the PDCA cycle.

Documenting lessons learned from the first pass

Also, in the previous Check phase of your cycle, you identified new knowledge, observations, and experiences that were noteworthy during execution of the project to date. Capturing this information through documentation will not only provide a solid reference for yourself and your project team during any future passes through this project, or on different project in the future, but it will provide a reference point to any re-planning effort so that it can be revisited during your next pass to ensure you are making progress that continually brings you closer to your goal.

Defining the scope of the needed changes

Once you have identified and documented what changes and/or additions you want to incorporate into your next PDCA cycle, with the information in hand you should run through the project management process in a condensed format to define the scope of the new work and ensure it is SMART. Once this is complete you can assess if your existing team and resources are adequate for the continuation of the work effort or if modifications are necessary to the composition of the project support structure as well.

Identifying the resources and time needed for any changes

Just like your initial effort at the beginning of your project, in consideration of your new scope to address the next pass at achieving the desired project outcomes, you will need to identify the resources available to complete the project work and determine the amount of time needed to perform each task. This will be quicker and more accurate this time around especially if you use a resource that completed work during your first pass, because you will be familiar with the way they work and the pace at which they could complete the assigned tasks.

Adjusting your project plan based on new information (first pass)

Revisit your original project plan and create a new version to incorporate the new activities needed to correct or address any outstanding issues. At this point you would push the project timeline forward to allow these activities to be completed in the new timeframe you have defined, but the placement of the activities within your project plan should be logically drawn to be an extension of where they should have been placed initially in the project plan. Knowing what you know now, where would you have placed the activity. Who would you have assigned the work to? How long would it have taken for the work to have been completed? And, how much would that line item have cost? These are all the questions you have to ask yourself at this stage, as you re-plan the missing components to your original project plan. Once you have completed your quick but thorough action plan, you will start your PDCA cycle again with all of the information you have at the ready and cycle through for another pass.

Round and Round We Go

At the point you have run through a complete pass at your project plan, all tasks have been completed and have produced a result that has allowed the next stage of the plan to keep moving forward and arrive at the last tasks being completed. You may think that since all the tasks are complete, that the project is over, but there is one final check to make against your project scope. This is the difference between producing a product or outcome, and producing the specific outcome or product defined in your scope.

Repeating the Plan, Do Check, Act Cycle

Going back to your project scope is coming full circle to check if what your team has produced meet the exact specifications. If you have defined in detail specific components that must be present in the final product, such as a car, a house, a certain measure of weight loss, specific business gains, or whatever outcome the project should have produced, now is your opportunity to compare what you have planned to what has been produced. Review your detailed project scope in view of what has been produced and ask yourself if the two are the same. If there are any differences between the two, now is the time to identify them. Define in detail what the difference is between what was planned and what you have as a product of the project work. If you are ok with the end product of the project work as it stands, even though there are discrepancies, then your project scope can be modified to match the final project outcome and any additional areas of the project plan like the budget, schedule, or other tasks can be adjusted likewise to mark the project work as complete. If you are not comfortable adjusting your project scope, then you can now review your project plan line by line to identify which activities would need to be performed again to modify and correct the project deficiencies.

PLAN - Assemble just the activities specifically related to the deficiencies, connect with the resources identified, and work as a team to develop a plan for completing the corrective measures. This will involve planning similar to the original project planning exercise, but on a much smaller scale. What is different here is that you are not working in isolation. You have to make adjustments in light of a result that already exists and make sure that any work that is done at this point can be covered by the contingencies you have initially set aside, in time and budget, and that doing this work will not negatively impact any other project component at this stage.

DO - Work closely with your team to begin the corrective measures and closely monitor their progress, clearing roadblocks along the way until they have arrived at the completion of the rework effort.

CHECK – Check the result of the corrective actions against your project scope and see if you have a match at this stage. If not, you need to go through another cycle again starting with identifying the discrepancies.

ACT – Make your decisions based on the previous cycle and either accept the result and move to close out your project, adapt to the new circumstance in this iteration and try again (going through the project plan again beginning at the re-planning effort), or abandon the project entirely.

That Magic Moment

Your most recent pass has been completed and you are reviewing the result. Everything lines up according to expectation and you get that warm fuzzy feeling inside. You feel overcome with joy as you are fairly certain your goal has been achieved. There are few moments in your life that feel as good as the day you complete your first project, and it only gets more emotional the bigger and better goals you achieve. Share your excitement with your team but save a little bit to make sure you are there.

All Tasks Completed

Review your project plan to make sure all planned activities have been completed from all passes and re-scoping instances, and results documented. If you have previously confirmed each task has achieved its objective, great, but if not, now would be the time to review. If everything looks good and is well documented, move to the next step.

Scope Has Been Achieved

Look back at your current SMART scope document and compare what is defined in the scope to the result of project work which is in front of you. Does the project outcome match what was defined in your project scope? If so, your project is almost complete. If not exactly matching, decide if you are willing to live with any differences that are present. If you are happy with the end product as virtually identical, then you have achieved your goal.

Quality Check Completed

Again, quality is a measure of the way something behaves and how it is achieved. Are you happy in the way in which the project outcome has been achieved, and does the end product live up to the expectation in that way it will be used? A final quality check to determine if the usefulness of the end result will meet expectations, as well as how well the project team and manager have performed in meeting the objectives is a useful tool for improvement.

Closing the Project

There are two instances where you would begin the closing process of your project. The first instance is when a project is humming along toward successful completion. Closing a running project is typically started when 90-95% of project tasks are complete. Throughout the project management cycle, you have been checking the completion of tasks to make sure the product of each tasks meets the quality or expected performance level. When it does not, you have acted to adjust your plan or project parameters to keep moving toward your goal. When the vast majority of tasks have been completed, meeting the expectation, you can begin the process of closing out your project. You want to be very hands on at the end of the project to keep your resources and yourself motivated and excited about achieving your goal. The second is closing a failed or dead project. There are many reasons why projects fail, from the timing not being ideal, running out of time or money, the lack of needed resources, or other reasons. If the project has been started and not finished, there is still value in closing the project properly to capture data, knowledge, specific circumstance, and lessons that have been learned within the failed project. Many past failed projects have been re-planned, resurrected and successfully completed during more favorable circumstances, at different times or with different resources, so it is always good to take every effort as an opportunity to learn.

Final closing tasks

When managing a project, the monitoring and checks performed on completed tasks gives you an indication of the progress you are making toward completion. In the Plan, Do, Check, Act cycle, you begin closing when the list of tasks to do is almost complete and the Checks are producing results that meet the expectation. These indicators prepare you for the right time to begin your closing tasks. The four closing tasks are as follows:

- Administrative closure – includes the releasing of project resources, completion of any final project related paperwork, making final payments, and capturing the final project budget values
- Contract closure – involves reviewing and resolving any outstanding contract issues with product or service providers, and closing any outstanding contracts
- Ending all project activities – involves verifying that all activities are complete and the project has produced its intended final product, service, goal, or outcome.
- Documentation – includes capturing important project information about your resources, the financial performance of your project, the accuracy of planning (planned versus actual), and even your performance managing the project.

Go through all of the areas of your project to identify any loose ends that have not been fully closed out from the categories above, resolve the issue and communicate the resolution to any involved parties, and document the final outcome as needed. Closing tasks entail a quick review and resolution process but communication and documentation remain important aspects to closing out your project.

Documenting What You Have Learned

You have already been documenting lessons learned from each pass through the PDCA cycle and now is your final review to ensure everything you have learned has been captured, including your successful final pass. Compile your observations, information and knowledge in your project folder, binder, computer file or other holder of project information and check for completion.

About your team performance

Team performance is often overlooked in getting project work done but as I have said before, your team is the life blood of your project. Having a great project team is an essential component because you cannot do all of the work and bear all of the responsibility yourself. Teams that work well are reflective of a great project manager, so reviewing the performance of your team on this project is looking into the mirror and seeing how well you did as a manager. Did the team communicate well? Did the team stay motivated? Did the team provide valuable input into the project planning and execution stages of the work? Was the team effective and efficient at meeting their goals? Did they stick to the project schedule and budget? As we answer these questions, they allow us to assess each team member and also review our own performance so that we can learn to be better.

About the project scope

Given what you know now at the completion of the project, was the scope actually SMART? If you had known what you know now at the beginning of the project, how would you have scoped it out differently? Defining the scope of a project is such a vital first step that getting it right the first time is a great skill to master. This can only be seen at the completion of a project, so gather this knowledge in preparation for the next step in your development.

About your budget

Crunching the project numbers, especially your budget, is important for new managers to develop tools and techniques to more accurately plan out project costs during the planning stages of a project. Planning is performed somewhat in a bubble and even if you get information from outside parties, looking at the accuracy of the information you were provided in retrospect is a good idea. Whatever happened in your project, were the costs accounted for in the worst case scenario and was there sufficient contingency set aside to account for the great unknown? This is like a crash course in economics and budgeting, but in the end you will become more accurate and thoughtful to this vital component of the iron triangle.

About the time you gave to the project

Another vital component of the iron triangle, the time you allotted to the tasks and the overall project timeline, must be dissected religiously to reveal the secrets within. Not only will your analysis of the timeline reflect your skills at scheduling and determining the duration of individual tasks, but it will also give clues and data that will provide insight into the performance of your human resources. Were people sick more than you expected? Did a resource's regular responsibilities draw them away from project work? Did a resource complete their activities quickly and then coast to take full advantage of the duration void allotted without contributing any additional effort? Also, capturing events that affected your timeline that were not originally planned can be useful as well, especially if there is a possibility of similar events impacting other similar projects in the future. For example, rolling blackouts in major city centers during extremely hot summers is an event that may become more regular with the changing global climate. If a rolling blackout prevented work from being completed, then take note. The same event may have also impacted other areas of your project such as materials, delays from third parties, additional costs for temporary power generation equipment, and so on.

About your performance as a PM

Now is the time to look in the mirror and take an honest look at how you performed. Were you a superstar in your own mind alone, or did your team genuinely think you were a great manager. There are two ways to look at the performance issue, the first is managing to achieve your goal in the project, and secondly managing your team effectively to perform well under the circumstances. If the stars aligned on your project and everything went well to allow you and your team to achieve your goal in the first pass, this would be fantastic! But would your team hate working for you as a project manager? Achieving a project outcome alone is not a great way to gage your project management skills. It is a blend of people management and performance toward achieving a goal. Looking back at your project documentation will provide insight on how well you did achieving the project outcome, but talking to your project team after the project is complete (perhaps in a 360 review format) is invaluable to providing input on how they viewed you as a leader. If you have cultivated an open and honest communication environment throughout your project, then you can expect good feedback on your performance from your team. Take the good comments with the bad and thank the team for their comments at the end. You will be a better leader by listening and learning from how others perceive you.

What would you have done differently if you knew then what you know now

After everything you have reviewed, learned, and dissected throughout this process, reflect back on your project and detail what you would have done differently with the information you know now. Hindsight always being 20/20, this not only provides a critical tool for assessing your planning and management skills, but it will help you anticipate in greater detail on your next project. Introspective learning is always to be welcomed.

Things will only get better

Projects need to be managed to be fully understood. No amount or theoretical knowledge can ever develop the knowledge that can be gained by actually performing the role of a project manager. Just like an armchair quarterback will never know what the pressure of 40,000 pairs of eyes has on your ability to throw a ball, an armchair project manager, team member or outside observer will never know the day to day challenges of a project manager. But one thing is for certain, we always improve. The profession and practice of project management is centered on continuous improvement and refinement, so as you complete more projects, you will get better and better at it. You will be able to look at objects in your daily life and things in the news, and relate them back to project work, breaking them down in your mind and exercising your mental muscles. Only then will you begin to realize how many projects are out there being run in a broad and varied number of industries, professions, companies, and fields of study around the globe. Take a moment to enjoy your new perspective and then get on with tackling your next big project … for YOU.

Party Time

Finally, after successful completion of a project, it is customary to have a gathering or party, not only to celebrate the success of the project but to give special thanks to the people, companies and resources involved in the overall effort. People are the life blood of projects as they are in the trenches completing the work. It is important to recognize their contributions and celebrate their involvement. Publically recognizing your team and specific members for their contribution is a special experience in both professional and personal life. The praise you highlight will instill confidence in your team members. Remember though that nothing replaces a personal heartfelt thank you to each individual that contributed to the success of your project. Taking time out to connect with them personally, thanking them, giving them positive observations of specific activities you noticed that they excelled at, and making them feel special is something they will remember. It will set you apart from impersonal and blanket corporate demonstrations of thanks. Take the opportunity to connect with your team and thank each member personally. It is a very fulfilling experience.

Celebrate with your team, thank them for their hard work, and to give them an idea of what you plan to do for your next project, to gauge if any of your team members want to take it to the next level and go around with you again on your next project. New projects tend to stem from completed projects and successful projects attract positive attention and lead to more and better opportunities. Celebrate your successes with an eye to the future and remember, it isn't a party unless there is cake!

Life Transformation – Final Thoughts

Lies, falsehoods, and mistruths being thrust in front of us every day. They offer promises of a better life, but in reality they serve only to take what you have. Your hard earned money, your freedom, your choices, and most importantly your time. I hope that through the course of reading this book, you have come to recognize the lies in your life and begin the process of reclaiming your own success. You do not have to be a superhero or prodigy to set yourself apart from the pack. You only need to act consistently using knowledge and tools that are proven to work. Everyone needs support, especially when they have chosen to tempt fate and grab hold of the lion's tail to achieve something unique, and this book is the beginning of the support I am offering to you.

Through the first two parts of this book, we have travelled together along a path to life change using tried, tested, and true, tools, techniques, processes and principles of project management. Just like project management has and will continue to transform the world we live in, its application to the challenges and aspirations in your life can deliver the results to transform it into the life you have always dreamed of living.

If you have worked diligently through the first two sections of this book, you will have the basic tools to venture out and achieve any of the dreams and goals you have identified on your strategic planning worksheets. In Part I of this book, you completed an exercise to identify the "starting point" from which your personal path of transformation would begin. We all have to start from somewhere and every individual's starting point will be different. Some people will have advantages in their lives and others will be disadvantaged. All of us however can achieve greatness and the satisfaction of knowing we can make our own dreams a reality.

You Are Not Alone

I truly believe that everyone, at any stage in their lives, at any age, in every country, and in every environment, can benefit from the application of simple project management tools and techniques in their personal lives. As you continue to explore the application of this knowledge to the achievement of your own dreams, remember that you are not alone. Whatever your personal network or level of connection between family, friends, loved ones, people you interact with daily or even people around the world, we are all travelling on a mutual journey through our lives in this shared moment. In as much as you feel motivated to transform your life, there are other people looking to better themselves as well. Working with a network of like-minded individuals looking to transform any similar aspect of their lives can not only be the push you need to get started, but an opportunity to share personal experiences and knowledge to keep you focused on reaching your goal.

Let me just reiterate one thing about our daily reality. You may have felt at various points in the reading or completion of exercises within this book that your employer is taking advantage, and in some instances you may be right, but understand that the goal of this book is not to have employees develop a distain for employers. There are good employers and not so good employers, and it is a sincere hope of mine that employers look to the knowledge within this book to empower and support their employees. Having spoken in front of many employee groups at the request of their employers to help create better work environments, it is clear that many good companies value their employees enough to work toward a better work culture. Having happy and motivated people participating in any workplace is an extremely valuable commodity in any industry, and supporting, facilitating, and empowering employee goals in their professional and personal lives should be the goal of every employer. It not only builds a strong workforce, but sparks innovation, enhances communication, promotes teamwork, creativity, and loyalty. The relationship between employer and employee can be so much more, one of mutual respect and support. My hope is that all employers work toward building great relationships with their work families.

Occupation and other elements of our daily lives has sold us on the idea that we are being more efficient, we can communicate vast amounts of information and coordinate with many people on a day to day basis, but we all still need to be hugged, held, embraced, kissed, to hear our loved ones voices live, and to see our children's faces. Not even the best technology of the day can capture a single moment of these elements of human interaction, and no person, company, or employer should deny us of that which makes us human. Making time to reconnect with those around you will take time, but trust me when I say it is a worthy endeavor to pursue.

Legacy

Sitting down with your children at any age and being open and honest about your successes, challenges, and failures, and transmitting knowledge of your own personal struggles and life experiences, only provides them with additional choices and opportunities for success. Teaching children at any age about an organized way of tackling a problem or working toward a goal can be an invaluable asset in their education as well as in their lives. As you endeavor to change your life through this book or by any means, involve your children or your family in the process. It will be a valuable learning experience for them and another opportunity for you to connect with them on a deeper level.

The Future Looks Bright

I am humbled by where our journey has taken us and am hopeful that by passing along the knowledge, principles, tools, and experience that project management has delivered to the world, you will be emboldened to take a step into the light and reach for a better future. Change always begins in the hearts and minds of people and is fueled by the path forward. Acknowledge that you have a history which has brought you to where you are today in all its positive and negative forms, but know that your history does not define your future. So go out and challenge the world to deliver to you the future you decide.

Control over your life

Early in this book, I walked you through a few simple techniques you can use to free up your time, money, and resources to give you the breathing room to work through the remainder of this book. As you have progressed through to this point, you have completed exercises and projects that will give you increasing levels of control over your life. Never stop pursuing and maintaining freedom and control over your life because over time more forces will continue to test and try and break through your defenses to recapture control over you and take whatever they can from your future. It is a constant battle and we must remain vigilant for the sake of our families and our future. This is your legacy.

You have covered a lot of ground as we approach the end of our time together, and you should be feeling motivated and empowered by your new found knowledge to create a world and a life that you can feel proud. Remember that you have already accomplished what very few people in this world will ever do. You have begun to take control over your life and become truly free.

Transforming the World

Connor Pierce has been delivering project management knowledge around the globe for many years through speaking engagements, providing expert advice, mentoring, coaching, and his business consulting practice. This book though is special because it is designed to help anyone who wants to make a change in their life with real skills they can use for a lifetime. At the completion of writing this book, Connor wanted to create an ongoing vision for updating and providing readers with new tools and techniques in project management, real world success stories that are evolving right now, and provide additional support to every reader to ensure they never feel alone again.

Over the next year, Connor will be creating several new channels to support his readers. They will include: a regularly updated website, Facebook page and Twitter feed; a series of YouTube videos that will supplement the knowledge in this book with content from his public speaking engagements; new templates, forms, and worksheets; and interesting case studies and stories from real readers detailing their personal life transformations. All of these channels will be registered on Google as they are created using the search terms "Transform your Life Guidebook" and "Connor J Pierce Author".

You should always feel welcome to contact Connor through these channels to let him know your personal story of challenge and triumph, request a speaking engagement, or inquire about additional avenues of support for achieving your dreams. He is always grateful to hear how his work has touched real people and transformed their lives. In addition to his busy public speaking schedule and ongoing business engagements, Connor sets aside whatever time he can to host special events specifically aimed at helping young people create success in their lives. Sharing his knowledge with young future leaders is personally important to him as it opens the door to a better future for all of humankind.

Concluding Remarks

Although our journey together has now come to any end, I would consider this a new and wonderful beginning for you. You now have the skills and knowledge to venture out into the world and achieve whatever your imagination can dream up. You now know how to conceptualize, plan, execute, and deliver a project to a successful conclusion. And hopefully, through the warm reception of your family, friends, and loved ones, you can begin building living a life with a singular focus and purpose of setting yourself and those around you free.

The knowledge that you documented, exercises you completed, and projects you have planned and worked through will provide you with the beginning of a legacy file that will grow over time to document your transformation. Also, this book can be referenced and shared with friends and family to provide useful insight and direction into their own lives. It is my sincere hope that through this book you are able to forge deeper relationships with the ones you love and that you are able to achieve endless happiness in your life. And finally, share your knowledge. Become a leader in your own life and help transform the world into a better place.

I truly thank you for picking up this book and reading it through. If you have gained any new knowledge from it, then it was worth it. Go forth and achieve!

Project Templates
and
Support Material

PM Journal

Know Thyself

Write down your greatest fears, deepest darkest secrets, biggest personal failures, and any other things that you have lied about, cheated on, or done wrong. Consider this your personal confession and initiation into a new life in which you will be totally honest with yourself on a daily basis. Take as much time as you need to write a complete list of all of your transgressions, fears, thoughts that you have not shared with anyone but yourself, until it is all on this page. If you need more space, add a blank lined page and keep writing until it is complete.

_____

_____

_____

_____

_____

_____

_____

_____

_____

_____

_____

_____

_____

_____

_____

_____

_____

_____

_____

_____

_____

_____

_____

_____

_____

_____

_____

_____

Once you are finished your list, find a quiet place away from anyone or anything that may distract you and **review your list by reading it aloud**. Feel the words as if they are coming from the emotions that generated them onto the page. After reading the last item on the list, take a few minutes to let them echo in your mind until their sound dissipates.

<u>Know Thyself (continued)</u>

It is at this point that you will take the pages from this form and any additional pages you have added to it; go to your backyard, front lawn, barbeque, local park with camping facilities or anywhere else in the great outdoors. With a lighter or matches, light the pages on fire until they are entirely engulfed in flames and watch them burn until they are entirely gone. As you watch the pages burn, let all of the negativity and weight on your mind and soul burn with it until it is entirely lifted away, leaving you with a clean slate to begin rebuilding yourself with complete honesty and light.

Once the pages have been destroyed, make this solemn vow to yourself.

"I solemnly vow never to reflect on these negative events in my life again, and if these thoughts do come into my mind, I will prominently remember that those components of my life are dead, burned, buried and gone, to live no more in my mind, heart, and soul."

Retirement Calculation

Complete the form below and follow the prompts to calculate your retirement nest egg value.

(1)   Years between your current age and retirement: _____ years ● **(A)**

(2)   Your hourly wage: $_____ per hour ● **(B)**

(3)   Daily hours worked: _____ hours per day ● **(C)**

(4)   Number of hours worked per week: _____ per week ● **(D)**

(5)   Number of hours worked per year: _____ per year (Value of **(D)** x 52) ● **(E)**

(6)   Annual earnings before tax: $_____ per year (Value of **(E) x (B)**) ● **(F)**

(7)   Total wages remaining before retirement: $_____ (Value of **(A) x (F)**) ● **(G)**

(8)   Your taxation rate including deductions: _____ % ● **(H)**

For your tax and deduction percentage, you will divide the money left over after all deductions by the full value of your pay for the period. For example, if you worked 80 hours over the last 2 weeks at an hourly rate of $25.00 per hour, your earnings are $2000.00 before tax and deductions. If your pay after all tax and deductions is $1500.00, then your calculation will look like this:

$1500.00 / $2000.00 = 0.75   Now take this value and subtract 1

0.75 – 1 = -0.25 Now take his negative value, change it to positive and multiply by 100.

-0.25 x 100 = -25   and changed into a positive number is 25.

This final number is your tax rate including deductions, which in our example is **25%**. This is an important rate to know as this represents the amount of money you earn that you do not have direct access to due to source deductions.

(9)   Taxes including deductions you will pay from now until retirement: $_____
        (Value of **(G) x (H)**) ● **(I)**

(10)   Money earned from now until retirement, after source deductions: $_____
        (Value of **(G) – (I)**) ● **(J)**

This final value is all the money that you will make between now until your retirement, given that everything remains the same. This is all the money you will have access to in order to buy a home, purchase transportation, have a family, travel, and all the other daily and landmark activities you are planning for within your lifetime. On the next page, you can take this one step further by deducting the value of key items so you can see how retirement will look.

Things You Want in Your Life

A Modest Home: $_____

For this value, you will search your local real estate market and find a home or condominium that appeals to you and that will meet your needs from now until retirement. Then you will double this value to account for the interest you will pay on a mortgage amortized over 25 years.

Annual Vacations: $_____

For this value, you will estimate roughly how much you will spend on an annual vacation and multiply this value by **(A)** which is the number of working years remaining before retirement.

A Family: $_____

The cost of a family will include: the cost of a Wedding and Honeymoon; and, $5,000 per year, per child from ages 0-18 years old (one child = $90,000)

Additional Information: $_____

At this point you can include any additional items that currently represent a lifestyle choice you would like to continue between now until retirement. For example, you could include values for eating out, entertainment, alcohol and cigarettes, or anything else that you foresee being an ongoing annual expense or a large expense such as a boat, a car, or other items on your wish list. Then you would take the sum of all of these additional items and multiply them by the number of years until retirement and insert this value above.

Total Value of Things You Want: $_____ **(K)**

CONCLUSION

At this point you are now able to reconcile the value for your earnings with the value of the things you want in your life, to see how things will look in retirement.

Subtract the value you have for **(K)** from **(J)**: $_____ **(L)**

This is how much money is left over at retirement.

Calculate your annual earnings minus source deductions by taking the value you have calculated for **(F)** and subtracting the source deduction percentage you calculated as **(H)**, and place the value here: $_____ **(M)**

Assuming that you will continue living in the same lifestyle, you will take the value of **(L)** which is the amount of money you have at retirement, and divide by **(M)** which is the value you have just calculated for your annual earnings minus source deductions, which will give you the number of years that you will be able to sustain yourself and your family in retirement years.

Number of Years of Retirement Living

(L) / (M) = _____

Remember: This is a basic exercise only taking into account essential factors to arrive at the number of years you will be supported in retirement. Factors that are not included here such as sales tax, meals, movies, clothing, furniture, utility and maintenance costs, cars, medical bills, insurance, and all other aspects of your daily life unaccounted for here will erode savings and those remaining number of years you are able to support yourself and your family in retirement.. If your final number at retirement is in negative numbers, meaning there is no income to sustain your life in retirement, let this be a wake-up call that firstly, you are not alone, and secondly you have time to change your circumstances to prepare and plan for a better future.

Employment Encroachment

Complete this worksheet over the period of a week to keep track of every instance that you have completed any form of work for your employer outside of your regularly defined working hours. Every phone call, conference call, email, overtime hour at home, the office or elsewhere, and the like, should be noted along with the amount of time you devoted to completing the task. Also, note every time you thought about something work related. For emails, a quick tip is for you to look at your sent box at the end of the week and note every email written or sent after hours. You could also CC yourself on after hour's emails and file them in a folder for the end of the week tally. (If you need additional space, feel free to print additional copies of this page or add a blank page.)

Start Date: _____
End Date: _____

DATE	TIME	BRIEF DESCRIPTION OF WORK	DURATION
		TOTAL TIME	

Employment Encroachment (continued)

DATE	TIME	BRIEF DESCRIPTION OF WORK	DURATION
		TOTAL TIME	

CALCULATE TOTAL VALUE OF EMPLOYER ENCROACHED TIME

_____ X _____ = _____
Total Time   Pay Rate   Lost Value

Total Taxes

Your current monthly income: $_____ (A)

Add the following tax values:

Your monthly tax and source deductions:	$_____
Property Tax	$_____
Tax on Investments	$_____
Business or Corporate Tax	$_____
Any other form of tax including sales tax	$_____
TOTAL TAXES	$_____ **(B)**

Your Total Effective Tax Rate: _____%

(Divide **(B)** / **(A)** and multiply by 100)

Exercise Notes:

_____
_____
_____
_____
_____
_____
_____
_____
_____
_____
_____
_____
_____
_____
_____
_____
_____
_____
_____

Fruits of Your Labor

Whether you are employed, unemployed, self-employed, run your own business or have another form of income, calculate your own buying power based on the criteria below. Should there be additional information that you would like to add, you can complete the additional information section provided for. At the completion of the exercise, jot down some basic notes about what you would change in light of the information provided that might increase your buying power in the future.

Your name: _____

Your current employer: _____ (or SELF)

Your current monthly income: _____ **(A)**

Your monthly tax and source deductions: _____ **(B)**

Monthly Start Value: $_____ ((A) – (B) income minus tax and deductions) **(C)**

Monthly Expenses:

Rent or Mortgage $ _____
Groceries $ _____
Transportation $ _____
Work Related Lunches Out $ _____
Work Related Dinners Out $ _____
Work Related Entertainment $ _____
Other work related items $ _____

    TOTAL EXPENSES $_____ **(D)**

Your Buying Power Before Sales Tax: $ _____ **(E)**
(Subtract **(C)** – **(D)** your total expenses from your monthly start value)

Your Local Sale Tax Rate: _____% Sales Tax Value: $_____ **(F)**

Your Buying Power After Sales Tax: $ _____
(Subtract **(E)** – **(F)** the value of your local sales tax rate from your total buying power)

Total Taxes Paid: $_____ **(G)**
(Add **(B)**+**(F)** your monthly tax and source deductions and sales tax value)

Your Effective Tax Rate: _____%
(Divide **(G)** / **(A)** and multiply by 100 to calculate your effective tax rate)

<u>Fruits of Your Labor (continued)</u>

Exercise Notes:

_____
_____
_____
_____
_____
_____
_____
_____
_____
_____
_____
_____
_____
_____
_____
_____
_____
_____
_____
_____
_____
_____
_____
_____
_____
_____
_____
_____

Finding the Time

Using the table below, document your activities during a 7 day week. Once you have completed your week, describing the activity, start and end times, duration, category, and priority, use a highlighter to mark only the Medium and Low priority activities.

Legend:

Day – Day of the week

Time – Start time of the Activity

Duration – Length of time in minutes to complete the Activity

Activity Description – Brief description of the Activity

Category: Necessity – Natural events that sustain your physical existence

              Health – Health and Hygiene Activities

              Travel – Time used to travel (not compensated)

              Social – Time socializing (not compensated)

              Entertainment – Time spent entertaining yourself or others (not compensated)

              Religion, Hobbies, Other – Any other categories that describe a regular activity

Priority: High – An activity vital to your daily life

              Medium – An important activity but which could be rescheduled if needed

              Low – An activity that occupies your time but does not furthering your goals

Day	Time	Duration	Activity Description	Category	Priority

Day	Time	Duration	Activity Description	Category	Priority

List only the Medium Priority Activities here:

_____
_____
_____
_____
_____
_____
_____
_____
_____
_____
_____
_____
_____

Note ways to either have someone else help you perform the activity, delegate the activity to someone else entirely, or for you to perform that activity more efficiently through better scheduling, grouping, or any other possible ways of completing the activity faster.

_____
_____
_____
_____
_____
_____
_____
_____
_____
_____
_____
_____
_____
_____
_____
_____
_____
_____

List only the Low Priority Activities here:

_____
_____
_____
_____
_____
_____
_____
_____
_____
_____
_____
_____

Note ways to eliminate these activities entirely, and/or ways to transfer responsibility for these activities to someone else.

_____
_____
_____
_____
_____
_____
_____
_____
_____
_____
_____
_____
_____
_____

Conclusion: (document the specific times you have carved out of your schedule and commit to using this time, and ONLY, this time to complete the work contained within this book.)

_____
_____
_____

TOTAL TIME RECAPTURED: _____

Shared Effort

Choose an activity that you perform on a regular basis that is typically completed on your own, and time how long you take to complete the activity (the duration of that activity). A couple of examples may be folding laundry, grocery shopping, or prepping and cooking food in advance for your busy work week. Once you have timed how long it took you to complete the activity on your own, log the activity and time below.

Activity Description: _____

Working Alone

Start Time: _____

End Time: _____

Duration: _____

Before completing the same activity the next time, ask one family member, friend, roommate, or any other person to help you perform the task. Once you have provided them with brief instruction on how to complete the task and what you are looking for as a final outcome, time how long completing the activity took with help. Once you have the second time, log it below and calculate how much time, if any, you saved in the performance of the activity by sharing the effort with another person.

Working with a Friend

Start Time: _____

End Time: _____

Duration: _____

TIME DIFFERENCE: _____

This saved time represents time that you have recaptured in your life. Feel free to apply this to a variety of activities in your daily life and gage the difference and additional benefit available by splitting your effort.

<u>Unplug</u>

Choose as many influencers, or distractions as you feel comfortable with and restructure your life for a set period of time to avoid their effect. You may want to start with a few hours in the evening, or on a weekend day, but do what you can to shut out the time killers.

List which distractions (time killers) you will try to eliminate for this exercise:

_____

_____

_____

_____

_____

_____

_____

_____

_____

Date: _____

Start Time: _____

End Time: _____

Notes on your experience:

_____

_____

_____

_____

_____

_____

_____

_____

_____

_____

_____

_____

_____

<u>Rediscover</u>

Connect with someone, either a person you have not spoken to in a long time or even a complete stranger – document the experience, how did it go down, where were you, how did you approach the situation, how did it make you feel before, during and after the experience, and what was memorable about it.

Notes on your experience:

_____

_____

_____

_____

_____

_____

_____

_____

_____

_____

_____

_____

_____

_____

_____

_____

_____

_____

_____

_____

_____

_____

_____

_____

_____

_____

_____

<u>Reconnect</u>

Make a short list of the important people in your life, friends, loved ones, etc. and schedule time over the next week to systematically touch base with each person by voice or in person to catch up with what is going on in their lives and share what is going on in yours. Reconnect and jot down some quick details below about the experience. Feel free to add a page or print a few extra copies of this page if you run out of space.

Who: _____

When: _____

How (method of contact): _____

Notes on your experience:_____

_____

_____

_____

Who: _____

When: _____

How (method of contact): _____

Notes on your experience:_____

_____

_____

_____

Who: _____

When: _____

How (method of contact): _____

Notes on your experience:_____

_____

_____

_____

Who: _____

When: _____

How (method of contact): _____

Notes on your experience:_____

_____

_____

_____

Mindfulness

Make time for yourself over the next week to use what you learned about unplugging from the world, and do something for you and you alone, with no distractions, totally focused on the task at hand. The task you choose could be anything you want and should take a minimum of 2 hours to complete, and a maximum of whatever time you feel you are comfortable with remaining unplugged. Remember, no distractions from the outside world. No cellular phones, TV, media conferring devices, or time killers whatsoever.

Start Date & Time: _____

End Date & Time: _____

Activity for YOU: _____

Notes on your experience:

_____
_____
_____
_____
_____
_____
_____
_____
_____
_____
_____
_____
_____
_____
_____
_____
_____
_____
_____
_____
_____
_____
_____
_____

Making Friends

Actively explore things happening in your life where people are getting together:

- Parties
- Group trips with a tour
- Night outs
- Church
- Work gatherings
- Events
- Community center programs
- Groups and clubs you can join
- Volunteering for charity work
- Etc.

List them all along with the frequency in which they meet.

Activity Description	Frequency

Choose one short term gathering, like a party or event, one medium term activity (max 8 weeks) like a course, and one long term activity like volunteer work, that will expand your network of friends and colleagues. Work them into your schedule and starting with the short term activity through to the long term activity; engage in the social activities you have chosen from your list.

Remember that building your network not only enhances your life, it opens you up to other ways of thinking and provides access to opportunities that you may not have had.

Principled Living

Starting from your current state in the areas described, you will identify what you would like that area of your life to look like in its ideal sense, as defined in your mind.

Relationships: _____
_____
_____
_____
_____
_____
_____
_____

Health and Physical Wellbeing: _____
_____
_____
_____
_____
_____
_____
_____

Emotional Wellbeing: _____
_____
_____
_____
_____
_____
_____
_____

Work Life: _____
_____
_____
_____
_____
_____
_____
_____

Finances: _____

_____

_____

_____

_____

_____

_____

All Other Areas: _____

_____

_____

_____

_____

_____

_____

_____

_____

_____

_____

Path Markers: _____

_____

_____

_____

_____

_____

_____

_____

_____

_____

_____

_____

_____

_____

_____

Simple Group Statements: _____

_____
_____
_____
_____
_____
_____
_____
_____
_____
_____
_____
_____
_____
_____
_____
_____
_____
_____
_____
_____
_____
_____
_____
_____
_____
_____
_____
_____
_____
_____
_____
_____
_____
_____
_____
_____
_____

Health Now - Daily Worksheet

Date: _____   Start Weight: _____

Wake Time: _____   Sleep Time: _____

Overall Feeling - Notes:

On Waking: _____

At Lunch: _____

At Bedtime: _____

Major Meals and Snack Info:

Breakfast: Time - _____   ☐ Healthy   or   ☐ Unhealthy
    Where: _____   With Whom: _____

Lunch: Time - _____   ☐ Healthy   or   ☐ Unhealthy
    Where: _____   With Whom: _____

Dinner: Time - _____   ☐ Healthy   or   ☐ Unhealthy
    Where: _____   With Whom: _____

Snacks: Time - _____   ☐ Salty   or   ☐ Sweet

Snacks: Time - _____   ☐ Salty   or   ☐ Sweet

Snacks: Time - _____   ☐ Salty   or   ☐ Sweet

Drink Info:	1	2	3	4	5	6	7	8	9	10	
Glasses of Water:	☐	☐	☐	☐	☐	☐	☐	☐	☐	☐	
Pop – Cans or Bottles:	☐	☐	☐	☐	☐	☐	☐	☐	☐	☐	
Coffee or Tea:	☐	☐	☐	☐	☐	☐	☐	☐	☐	☐	
Alcohol:	☐	☐	☐	☐	☐	☐	☐	☐	☐	☐	Specify: _____
Cigarettes or Pipe:	☐	☐	☐	☐	☐	☐	☐	☐	☐	☐	Specify: _____
Drugs:	☐	☐	☐	☐	☐	☐	☐	☐	☐	☐	Specify: _____

Hours worked: _____   **Relaxation Time:** _____
(Include time both at work or outside of work, i.e. checking emails, thinking about work related items, etc.)

Hours of TV watched: _____

Time spent deliberately exercising: _____   **Type of exercise:** _____

Health Now – Consolidated Worksheet (1 Week)

Date: _____   **Average Weight:** _____

Average Wake Time: _____   **Average Sleep Time:** _____

Average Feelings - Notes:

On Waking: _____

At Lunch: _____

At Bedtime: _____

Major Meals and Snack Info:

Breakfast: Average Time - _____   Total Number of Healthy Meals: _____
    Predominantly Where: _____   Total Number of Unhealthy Meals: _____
    Predominantly With Whom: _____

Lunch: Average Time - _____   Total Number of Healthy Meals: _____
    Predominantly Where: _____   Total Number of Unhealthy Meals: _____
    Predominantly With Whom: _____

Dinner: Average Time - _____   Total Number of Healthy Meals: _____
    Predominantly Where: _____   Total Number of Unhealthy Meals: _____
    Predominantly With Whom: _____

Average Number of Snacks per day: _____

Total Number of Salty Snacks per week: _____

Total Number of Sweet Snacks per week: _____

Drink Info:

Average number Glasses of Water per day: _____

Average number of Cans or Bottles of Pop per day: _____

Average number of cups of Coffee or Tea per day: _____

Average amount of Alcohol per day: _____ Type: _____

Average number of Cigarettes or Pipe per day: _____ Type: _____

Average amount of Drugs consumed per day: _____ Type: _____

Average hours worked per day: _____ **Average relaxation time per day:** _____
Average hours of TV watched per day: _____
Average time exercising per week: _____ **Type of exercise:** _____

Our Food – Grocery Shopping Checklist

This exercise will begin with a trip to the supermarket and a permanent marker. Let's begin with a brief primer about supermarket layout. Typically a supermarket is laid out to have basic fresh and frozen foods on the outside walls of the building and foods that are processed in the center aisles. Without knowing how much you spend on groceries per week or what specifically you purchase, we will design rules that can be easily applied to everyone's shopping lists and to keep you in control of the choices of products. So here is what you will need to do to prepare for our exercise:

- ☐ The preference is to begin this process on a weekend day. Either day will do.

- ☐ With your total budget value for this shopping trip, separate 80% and 20% of the dollar value.

- ☐ With the 80% you will only by items from the fresh areas of your supermarket, excluding the bakery. This will include fresh fruits, vegetables, meats, cheeses, fish, and dairy (excluding items with sugar added).

- ☐ The remaining 20% can be spent on anything else in the store, but should include at least 2 cases of six 1.5 liter bottles of water.

- ☐ When you arrive home and unpack your groceries, you will mark each item with a symbol or your initials so that they can be easily identified and then pack them away in their normal place in your kitchen. Let any other family members or others with access to the kitchen know that they should not use anything marked with your special symbol or initials.

- ☐ For the bottles of water, minimum of 12 in total, you will mark them with the numbers 1 and two so that you have 6 sets of 2 water bottles.

Our Food – Weekly Challenge

Using the information from the Food and Drink section of your consolidated worksheet, identify the following information:

- Average Wake time
- Average Sleep time
- Times that breakfast, lunch and dinners are eaten

I will list some simple rules for you to incorporate into your daily life for a period of one week and then we will reference our numbers to see what has changed.

And here is my set of pilot rules for you to stick to for one week, using only the items you purchased on your shopping list. You can print off this list and take it with you so that you can reference the rules throughout the day and check them off as you achieve each rule within the day. Here we go:

- ☐ Within 30 minutes of waking, drink 1-2 glasses of water.
- ☐ Within 1 hour of waking, eat breakfast. Breakfast must include protein in any form you like.
- ☐ Avoid adding salt to any meals or snacks.
- ☐ Only drink caffeinated drinks in your home or at your workplace. Pick one place only.
- ☐ When leaving your home for work, take one set (marked 1 and 2) of water bottles.
- ☐ Between the time you leave your home and the time you go to bed, you will do your best to drink the water in both 1.5 liter bottles of water (3 liters in total).
- ☐ Any snacks you eat must be from the items you bought at the supermarket i.e. no outside snacks.
- ☐ Lunch can be anything you want from the items bought at the supermarket or from any outside source like a restaurant, café, office lunch, etc. but must be at least half comprised of vegetables grown above ground i.e. not potatoes or root vegetables.
- ☐ Dinner should be the last thing eaten in your day and should contain less than ¼ of protein. It can be eaten from items purchased at the supermarket or can be outside food, just be aware if ordering in a restaurant, to let the server know the proportions of protein to other items on the plate so that they can help guide your choice to meet those proportions.
- ☐ No alcohol or caffeinated beverages should be consumed after eating dinner.
- ☐ Dinner should be eaten at least 2 hours before going to sleep.
- ☐ Just before bed, drink at least one glass of water.
- ☐ Feel free to take notes throughout the week of any positive or negative things you notice.

That's it!!   Follow this routine for one week and complete the results page.

<u>Our Food – Weekly Challenge - Results</u>

Answer the following questions to see what has changed during your week long food exercise:

Has your weight changed: ☐ Yes   or   ☐ No

    Start Weight: _____

    Current Weight: _____

    Difference: _____

Did you ever feel starved of food: ☐ Yes   or   ☐ No

How do you feel generally: _____

_____

_____

_____

_____

_____

List any positive or negative changes you have noticed: _____

_____

_____

_____

_____

_____

What would you change in this routine to better suit your specific needs, to enhance the positive changes you noted and reduce the negative changes you listed: _____

_____

_____

_____

_____

_____

Is this routine list or your adjusted list sustainable over a long period:

        ☐ Yes   or   ☐ No

Physical Exercise

For this exercise, you will need to following information from your initial data sheet:

Start Weight: _____

Time Spent Exercising: _____

Type of Exercise: _____

General Overall Feeling

    On Waking: _____

    At Lunch: _____

    At Bedtime: _____

Using the same methodology of principled living, I will outline some basic rules to be incorporated into your daily routine for the next 7 days. Keep in mind that everyone is at different levels of fitness and if you feel uncomfortable at any point or unable to complete an exercise due to physical ailment, disability or injury that is totally ok. Just move on to the next item on the list. Here are the rules of this exercise:

- ☐ On waking and before bed, do any stretches you wish to at least 4 different body parts
- ☐ At least 3 days during the week, travel with a friend at least 15 minute by foot to eat your lunch. This could mean walking 15 minutes to a restaurant or café, or 15 minutes to a local park to enjoy your meal outside. In whatever form you choose, just make sure it is at least 15 minutes each way. Have fun with this by choosing an out of the way lunch destination and bringing a buddy with you.
- ☐ At least 4 days a week, go out for a leisurely stroll right after dinner for at least 30 minutes, preferably with a friend or loved one, but if it's just you and your music, that's ok too
- ☐ Whenever you see an escalator, treat it like the plague and take the stairs. (Now this one is only if you feel up to it. Not everyone has the same level of mobility, and if you are at all uncomfortable with doing this, by all means avoid it.)
- ☐ If you have a regular exercise routine, continue to follow your routine
- ☐ Feel free to take notes throughout the week of any positive or negative things you notice

That's it for this exercise. A basic, simple routine that is easy to incorporate into your week. Again you can print off this short list and put a checkmark beside each items as you complete it. Once you have completed the week, let's revisit the list from the data sheet.

Physical Exercise – Results

Has your weight changed, if so how much: _____

How do you feel generally: _____
_____
_____
_____
_____
_____
_____

List any positive or negative changes you have noticed: _____
_____
_____
_____
_____
_____
_____

What would you change in this routine to better suit your specific needs, to enhance the positive
changes you noted and reduce the negative changes you listed: _____
_____
_____
_____
_____
_____
_____

Is this routine list or your adjusted list sustainable over a long period:

☐ Yes   or   ☐ No

Additional Notes: _____
_____
_____
_____
_____
_____
_____

Methods of Escape

Vices come in many forms and can be affect us in many ways, but this simple approach will focus on reducing their impact for a short time to see what the effects are to your wellbeing.

Using the information from the initial data sheet, you will need the following information:

Number of sweet versus salty snacks consumed in a day, week: _____

Number of cans or bottles of pop, cups of coffee or tea a day: _____

Amount of alcohol consumed per day, week: _____

Number of cigarettes, cigars, pipe per day: _____

Number of hours of TV watched in a day: _____

Number of hours worked per day, week (both at work or outside of work): _____

Over the next 7 days, incorporate these basic rules into your daily routine. Here are the rules of this exercise:

- ☐ Follow the first two exercises while completing this exercise.
- ☐ Pick two days in the week that will be your cheat days. _____
- ☐ On the selected cheat days only, you can eat or drink any of the salty or sweet snacks, caffeinated drinks or alcohol, but only at the times indicated in exercise one.
- ☐ For smokers, set aside exactly half of what you would normally consume in a week into a separate container, be it a plastic sandwich bag, cigar or cigarette case of another suitable container. Feel free to smoke at any times you wish, but just budget your consumption to not exceed what you have set aside. You may want to also pack some gum along with your smoking products to give you a choice come the time.
- ☐ For users of illicit drugs, commit at least 2 hours during the week exploring the impact of drug use on your health and looking into available cessation programs or support groups in your area.
- ☐ On days other than your cheat days, on leaving your workplace, you will turn off your work related mobile device, leave your computer at your workplace and commit to not checking your emails or even thinking about work once you leave.
- ☐ Also, on days other than cheat days, spend at least an hour of time on each day, which would have been spent watching TV, reaching out and connecting by voice or face to face with a friend or loved one. Electronic mediums and social media are not an option.
- ☐ Feel free to take notes throughout the week of any positive or negative things you notice.

At the end of the week, review your initial data and let's see what has changed by completing the results page.

Methods of Escape - Results

How do you feel generally: _____
_____
_____
_____
_____

List any positive or negative changes you have noticed: _____
_____
_____
_____
_____

Have the changes you have made this week impacted any of the results from the other two exercises: _____
_____
_____
_____
_____

Did you save any money by reducing your consumption and if so, how much: _____
_____

What was the reaction from the people you connected with by voice or face to face: _____
_____
_____
_____

What would you change in this routine to better suit your specific needs, to enhance the positive changes you noted and reduce the negative changes you listed: _____
_____
_____
_____
_____

Is this routine list or your adjusted list sustainable over a long period:

☐ Yes   or   ☐ No

Ideal Health – CONCLUSIONS

From the results of our three brief exercises, review the results you have noted at the end of each exercise and determine the following:

What has changed both positively and negatively during the exercises: _____

_____

_____

_____

_____

_____

Looking at the positive and negative changes in the three key areas, which factors contributed to the positive changes and which factors contributed to the negative changes in each exercise: _____

_____

_____

_____

_____

_____

_____

List 3-5 ways you can promote or enhance each of the positive changes listed in your exercises and list 3-5 ways you can reduce or eliminate the negative changes listed in your exercises: _____

_____

_____

_____

_____

_____

Using your lists of enhancing the positive and reducing the negative changes exercise, develop a simple framework of rules that you can apply on a daily basis that would capture the essence of your lists as it would broadly apply to your life.

What have you learned about yourself during this exercise: _____

_____

_____

_____

_____

_____

_____

_____

Personal Retreat Workbook

Personal Retreat – Setting the Stage

There is no exact formula to delivering successful results within a personal or executive retreat, but there are things you can do to give yourself the opportunity to achieve a better outcome. Firstly, make sure to give yourself enough time. There is no deadline for completing this exercise, but there is a limited opportunity to ensure complete focus. The time allotted to your personal retreat should be adjusted to allow you to capture all the information you need to move forward, focus on you and redefine YOUR future. Some people can manage to complete this work in a few hours and others may take several weeks. Whatever time you set aside, your goal is to complete this work as comprehensively as possible.

Get away from everything and everyone, and going to a place that is entirely new and that you have never been to before will help you relax and focus on the work of life redesign. If there are other people around or some form of distractions, try to find a secluded place where you will have total peace and quiet and will be undisturbed.

When you need a mental or physical break, engage in some pampering or relaxation services to de-stress and return focus back onto yourself. Enjoy a casual stroll, a nature walk, a coffee or glass of wine on a restaurant patio, and enjoy the company of your own thoughts.

Once you have planned out the details of your personal retreat, capture the logistic information on the lines below, and also write down a few basic thoughts about your reason for completing this retreat at this point in your life and what you hope to focus your attention on during this exercise.

When? (start date): _____

(end date): _____

Where? (location): _____

Why? (reasons): _____

_____

_____

_____

_____

_____

_____

<u>Personal Retreat - Brainstorming</u>

Personal Retreat - Brainstorming

Personal Retreat - Brainstorming

Personal Retreat – Self-Assessment

Step 1 - Self-Assessment

List what you consider to be all of the most important areas in your life. Once you have listed them, go through your list and reorder the items according to priority with the most important at the top and the least important at the bottom. Once complete, this list will identify your personal Key Life Areas.

Most Important Life Areas:

_____

_____

_____

_____

_____

_____

_____

_____

_____

_____

_____

_____

_____

_____

_____

_____

_____

_____

_____

_____

_____

_____

_____

_____

Reordered List by Rank (High to Low):

_____

_____

_____

_____

_____

_____

_____

_____

_____

_____

_____

_____

_____

_____

_____

_____

_____

_____

_____

_____

_____

_____

_____

_____

Personal Retreat – Self-Assessment (cont'd)

Step 1 - Self-Assessment (cont'd)

List your current daily routine (typical day) in as much detail as possible, for one week day, and one weekend day.

Weekday Routine:

_____

_____

_____

_____

_____

_____

_____

_____

_____

_____

_____

_____

_____

_____

_____

_____

_____

_____

_____

_____

_____

_____

_____

_____

_____

_____

_____

_____

Weekend Routine:

_____

_____

_____

_____

_____

_____

_____

_____

_____

_____

_____

_____

_____

_____

_____

_____

_____

_____

_____

_____

_____

_____

_____

_____

_____

_____

_____

_____

Personal Retreat – Self-Assessment (cont'd)

Step 1 - Self-Assessment (cont'd)

Look at the two lists above side by side and identify connections between what you feel is most important in your life and what you do on a daily basis. Try to quantify the value of the items listed by time, effort, value, money, and whatever else you can use as a measure to identify how much the item is represented in your current daily routine. For example, if health and wellbeing is high on your list of Key Life Areas but your current daily schedule only has 30 minutes of exercise listed on a weekly basis; this would indicate a conflicting application of values.

The goal of this part of the exercise is to highlight how much of what you feel are the most important aspects of your life are reflected in your day to day routine, and identify areas where there is a perceived or real conflict in the values that you hold important, so they can be explored and resolved. Document your findings on this page.

_____
_____
_____
_____
_____
_____
_____
_____
_____
_____
_____
_____
_____
_____
_____
_____
_____
_____
_____
_____
_____
_____
_____
_____

Personal Retreat – Free Up Your Time

Step 2 – Find the time - Free up your time

Review the outcomes of your Work Life exercise on **Work Encroachment** and your Personal Life exercise on **Finding the Time** and identify 3-5 ways you can recapture at least 5 hours of your time each week (1 hour a day) to work on achieving your goals. Detail all of the different ways you have identified pockets of free time in your schedule, and the specific blocks of time that you have discovered by following the noted exercises. For each of the blocks of time you have identified, set a repeating calendar appointment with notification or reminders to reserve these times for your transformative work.

_____
_____
_____
_____
_____
_____
_____
_____
_____
_____
_____
_____
_____
_____
_____
_____
_____
_____
_____
_____
_____
_____
_____
_____
_____
_____
_____
_____
_____
_____

Personal Retreat – Defining Your Ideal Life

Step 3 – Defining your ideal life

Begin documenting key aspects of your life as they are now. Once complete, begin defining the same key aspect of your life in a way that captures the way you want it to be. For example, if I am currently 300 pounds, then I would put that figure under the physical health section of the template, and if I want to be 190 pounds at some future point, then I would place that figure beside my original weight in the ideal state column. Add more pages if needed.

Life Area 4 Key Areas	Current State	Future State	Size of Change (S/M/L)	Value of Change (High/Med /Low)	Time (Now/ Later/ Any time)	Total	Final Rank
Work Life							
Personal Life							
Relationships							
Health							

Personal Retreat – Defining Your Ideal Life (cont'd)

Step 3 – Defining your ideal life (cont'd)

This is your custom template in which you can capture details of additional areas of your life that do not necessarily fall within the Key Life Areas in the previous template. Here you are able to capture these specific details of your life that you would like to see change and identify its current and future state.

Life Area (Custom)	Current State	Future State	Size of Change (S/M/L)	Value of Change (High/Med /Low)	Time (Now/ Later/ Any time)	Total	Final Rank

Personal Retreat – Defining Your Ideal Life (cont'd)

Step 3 – Defining your ideal life (cont'd)

Final Ranked List of Life Change

Life Area	Current State	Future State	Final Rank

Personal Retreat – Commitment

Step 4 – Commit to change one thing that is important to you

A commitment is the deepest essence of who we are as individuals. It is a solemn promise to our own true self that we will execute our free will to perform an action or pursue a result unobstructed by any opposing force. Commitment to yourself that you will change at least one thing that is important to your life starting today. Write down your commitment in as much detail as possible.

_____

_____

_____

_____

_____

_____

_____

_____

_____

_____

_____

_____

_____

_____

_____

_____

_____

_____

_____

_____

_____

_____

_____

_____

_____

_____

Personal Retreat – Find the Resources

Step 5 – Find the Resources - Free up resources

Review your ranked list of goals and with your current network of connections in mind, work through each goal listed and link all the names of people that come to mind that you feel would be helpful in achieving each goal. When you work through this process, you may have names appearing in multiple places, and other areas where you have gaps. This is ok. Once you have made a complete first pass at your list, start from the top again looking at each item and adding to each list of names, the resources you will need to complete the project. They may not even be names, but could be a description of a resource like, lawyer, accountant, fitness instructor, realtor, or any other resource needed to ensure you reach that goal. Finally, match up the names of the resources you listed with the needed resources and identify which resources you are currently missing.

Goal: _____   Rank: _____

Mentors: _____

Your Resources: Needed Resources:

_____   _____
_____   _____
_____   _____
_____   _____
_____   _____
_____   _____
_____   _____
_____   _____
_____   _____

Resource Gaps:

_____   _____
_____   _____
_____   _____

Personal Retreat – Find the Resources (cont'd)

Step 5 – Find the Resources – Line 'em up! (cont'd)

Goal: _____ Rank: _____

Mentors: _____

Your Resources: Needed Resources:

_____   _____
_____   _____
_____   _____
_____   _____
_____   _____
_____   _____

Resource Gaps:

_____   _____
_____   _____
_____   _____

Goal: _____ Rank: _____

Mentors: _____

Your Resources: Needed Resources:

_____   _____
_____   _____
_____   _____
_____   _____
_____   _____
_____   _____

Resource Gaps:

_____   _____
_____   _____
_____   _____

Personal Retreat – Drawing Your Roadmap

Step 6 – Drawing your roadmap - Decide what you want to change first

Taking into account the information you discovered about the availability of needed resources to complete work on your transformative effort, document your final roadmap. This roadmap is an ordered list of the steps your will take and the projects you will design with my guidance, to begin transforming your life. Remember that your final list should consider if you have all of the needed resources to complete your goal, the time and environment in which you are working on achieving your goal, and the availability of a mentor that can help provide guidance to you throughout the process. Create your final list of goals here.

_____
_____
_____
_____
_____
_____
_____
_____
_____
_____
_____
_____
_____
_____
_____
_____
_____
_____
_____
_____
_____
_____
_____
_____
_____
_____
_____
_____

Scope Definition Worksheet

Defining the scope of your project below, you will capture a detailed idea or picture of what you are trying to accomplish, create, or build. Quantify in real terms the objectives your project will aim to achieve and define the approach you will take, the resources you have available or will recruit, give concrete numbers and dates to your success criteria, and list sources of information on other similar projects that have been completed along with the process used to achieve success. If you have tried to achieve this goal or similar goals before, write down the lessons you have learned from your previous attempt. You could also provide some details of any mentors that will be lending their support to you during this journey. Begin defining your scope here:

_____

_____

_____

_____

_____

_____

_____

_____

_____

_____

_____

_____

_____

_____

_____

_____

_____

_____

_____

_____

_____

_____

_____

_____

_____

_____

SMART Template

SMART is a principle used to help fully capture the scope of your goal (dream) and to ensure you have thought about essential requirements to define and conceptualize key aspects in preparation for planning your project to achieve your dream.

For each dream you will work to achieve, break down the following information from your Scope Definition Worksheet and provide as much detail below as possible.

S – Specific

Being specific about what you want to achieve, build, or create is a vital first step in the success of your project. Define your idea being as specific as possible. Ask yourself all the questions that will clarify your project scope such as: what you will accomplish; when will the project start and end; why do you want to accomplish this goal and why now; where will the work take place; who will be involved; how will you work to achieve your goal. At the end of this step, you should have a detailed image of what the outcome of your project should look like.

_____

_____

_____

_____

_____

_____

_____

_____

_____

_____

_____

_____

_____

_____

_____

_____

_____

_____

_____

_____

_____

_____

_____

M – Measurable

Measuring your progress to achieving success in anything over a period of time requires landmarks along the way. We need to define what landmarks are on the road we are travelling, that will indicate to us we are either on the right path or travelling in the right direction to reach our goal. Measures of success are the tangible aspects of your project that you can define and track your progress against. Ask yourself, how will you know when you have accomplished your goal? What are the measures of success? Identify targets to achieve by a certain time. Measures are control mechanisms that alert you to progress within your project and the work you have assigned to other resources, and provide feedback to give you time to make plan adjustments. Provide details on the tangible metrics of your project that can measure your progress. Questions to ask yourself could include: when; how many; what indicators; how much; what percentage.

_____

_____

_____

_____

_____

_____

_____

_____

_____

_____

_____

_____

_____

_____

_____

_____

_____

_____

_____

_____

_____

_____

_____

_____

_____

A – Achievable

Is your goal achievable and what steps are you planning to take to achieve that goal? Create a step by step list of all the ways possible that you can achieve your goal. You can tap other people for this as well by asking them what they did to achieve a similar goal, or even a portion of a goal. Take note that these steps are in a specific order of thinking and you should only think about the steps in their given order. To complete this step, you should not limit your list of ways to achieve a given goal by the resources needed or available, or limit your scope in step one by what you feel are limitations to what you are capable of. Open yourself up to the infinite possibilities, as this is capturing dreams without limits. If a path requires specific resources, list those resources and plan as if they are present.

_____
_____
_____
_____
_____
_____
_____
_____
_____
_____
_____
_____
_____
_____
_____
_____
_____
_____
_____
_____
_____
_____
_____
_____
_____
_____
_____
_____

R – Realistic

This is the step where you place your dream into a box that defines how long you will work on this dream, what resources are available to you, and how realistic achieving your goal is as defined. Can this goal be achieved given the current availability of resources, knowledge, and time? Identify the resources needed, budget, people, products, and stakeholders within this step.

_____
_____
_____
_____
_____
_____
_____
_____
_____
_____
_____
_____
_____
_____
_____
_____
_____
_____
_____
_____
_____
_____
_____
_____
_____
_____
_____
_____
_____
_____
_____
_____

Resources:

Being realistic about your project also means taking account of your available resources. Remember that you have been creative in identifying resources, but now is the time to take stock of what your reality looks like at this point in time. Reach out to identify what resources are actually available from your list of needed resources to complete your project. Identify gaps in key resources and consult all possible resources and people within your network to see how you can fill the gaps and if needed, the cost of doing so.

_____
_____
_____
_____
_____
_____
_____
_____
_____
_____
_____
_____
_____
_____
_____

Budget:

As with recruitment of resources, your budget is another constraint because it is a predetermined fixed value. All projects have limited resources and money is one of the key resources that can determine the success or failure of a project. Be realistic about exploring all paths to successfully complete your project and for each one you are seriously exploring, determine what the budget would be and where the budget would be allocated.

_____
_____
_____
_____
_____
_____
_____
_____

T – Time Based

This final step in our SMART assessment is applying a timeline to achieving the scope of your goal. No project lasts forever and, as we explained before, long projects promote the loss of focus and are very difficult to plan with any level of accuracy. Placing a timeline on your project allows you to define resources and the duration of tasks to work within the timeframe. When thinking about completing this step, ask yourself the question; when will the goal be accomplished? Reflect on all the other steps we have taken, all the people you have spoken to and all the knowledge you have gained to this point in defining the time you are allowing for completing your project. Make sure it's an informed figure and not just an unrealistic number of months or a broadly undefined value of "however long it takes". Define it here so that we can plan for it, and work toward it.

_____
_____
_____
_____
_____
_____
_____
_____
_____
_____
_____
_____
_____
_____
_____
_____
_____
_____
_____
_____
_____
_____
_____
_____

Scope Statement Worksheet

Project Title: _____

Summary: (concise description of what the project intends to do)

_____
_____
_____
_____
_____

Key Project Objectives: (key markers of project success)

_____
_____
_____
_____
_____
_____
_____
_____
_____
_____
_____
_____
_____

Assumptions and Constraints: (list any assumptions or constraints that may impact your project)

_____
_____
_____
_____
_____
_____
_____
_____
_____

Detailed Project Description: (elaborate on your concise description above)

_____
_____
_____
_____
_____
_____
_____
_____
_____
_____
_____
_____
_____
_____
_____
_____

Project Milestones: (target dates for completion of important components of the project)

_____
_____
_____
_____
_____
_____
_____
_____
_____
_____
_____
_____
_____
_____
_____
_____
_____
_____

Project Approach: (describe how you will approach the achievement of the project objectives)

_____
_____
_____
_____
_____
_____
_____
_____
_____
_____
_____
_____
_____

Budget: (provide an idea of the project costs, which will be revisited after planning)

_____
_____
_____
_____
_____
_____
_____
_____

Resources: (list all available resources for this project including people, money, time)

_____
_____
_____
_____
_____

Mentors: (provide information on project mentors)

_____
_____
_____
_____

Project Planning Workbook

Activity Definition Worksheet

Define as many activities with as much detail as possible into manageable chunks of work (work packages), and group similar and/or related activities together. Identify any gray areas that you know exist but that you have minimal or no knowledge or experience with, and try to define the general idea of the gray space. Talk to people with first-hand experience completing similar projects or project work and ask them if your list of activities related to their experience is complete, and add any detail based on their input. Do the same for any independent research or knowledge you are able to dig up from sources in the know. Refine your grouped list of activities to the lowest possible denominator that will represent a reasonable amount of time. At the completion of this exercise, you should have a concise yet detailed list of activities or tasks needed to achieve the project goal.

_____
_____
_____
_____
_____
_____
_____
_____
_____
_____
_____
_____
_____
_____
_____
_____
_____
_____
_____
_____
_____
_____
_____
_____

Activity Sequencing Worksheet

Go through your entire list of activities and make sure each item is in the right place. Simply ask yourself, what must I do first, and then what comes after that. Grouping related events can also help identify your sequence as you are better able to visualize how a smaller group of events or tasks may interact with each other, than a large list of tasks in a complex project. If you feel comfortable grouping a bunch of related tasks into modules and then sequencing the modules, then you can utilize this method. Just remember that some tasks in your modules may be related to or impact tasks in other areas of your project so keep in mind these connections. Also, tasks completed concurrently would impact the schedule only once.

Seq.#	Activity Description
1	
2	
3	
4	
5	
6	
7	
8	
9	
10	
11	
12	
13	
14	
15	
16	
17	
18	
19	
20	
21	
22	
23	
24	
25	
26	
27	
28	
29	
30	

Activity Duration Worksheet

Make another pass at your sequenced activity list adding how much time you think, or have calculated, each activity will take to complete. It is important to understand at this point all of the factors that may impact an activity to determine how long it will take to complete so that you can get a fairly accurate duration value. This is where it is important to talk to people with first-hand experience or special expertise with the activity to help provide you with accurate information. For tasks on your activity list that involve repetition, consider a time estimation tool taken from the concept of an assembly line, which provides a great way to determine fairly accurately the duration of a repetitive task, and also a good way to conceptualize a method of estimation that you can apply in many different ways to arrive at the length of time needed to complete a task.

Seq.#	Activity Description	Duration
1		
2		
3		
4		
5		
6		
7		
8		
9		
10		
11		
12		
13		
14		
15		
16		
17		
18		
19		
20		
21		
22		
23		
24		
25		
26		
27		
28		
29		
30		
	TOTAL TIME (Non-Concurrent Tasks)	

Activity Cost Worksheet

Determine the cost of each activity using a logical process involving the review of resources that will be doing the actual work to complete the task, assessing the cost of tools, supplies or other support systems needed by the resources, calculating time and costs related to overhead and delay (cost of waiting), and any other costs associated to the completion of an activity. If you are not sure what an activity would cost, get a quote. Your activity costs will add up to form your overall project budget, so if you have grouped activities within the initial planning process, you will be able to determine the costs associated to each group of related activities, the costs for each individual resource, material and equipment costs, and more. This information will become valuable if your scope changes or if unforeseen events crop up while your project is running.

Seq.#	Activity Description	Cost
1		
2		
3		
4		
5		
6		
7		
8		
9		
10		
11		
12		
13		
14		
15		
16		
17		
18		
19		
20		
21		
22		
23		
24		
25		
26		
27		
28		
29		
30		
	TOTAL COST	

Project Resource Planning Worksheet

At this point, with your activity list in hand, review the list to determine who or what resources are available to complete each task. Some tasks will require only people, others will require only tools or machines, and others will require both. Some activities can be completed by yourself, others may require a person you know, and yet others will require you to hire an expert or outside resource. What you are looking for when choosing a resource is a mix of the right person for the job who is capable of delivering the expected result from the activity, who is available when you need the work to be completed, and at a reasonable cost.

Seq.#	Activity Description	Resources
1		
2		
3		
4		
5		
6		
7		
8		
9		
10		
11		
12		
13		
14		
15		
16		
17		
18		
19		
20		
21		
22		
23		
24		
25		
26		
27		
28		
29		
30		

Individual Resource Planning Worksheet

To assign work to individual resources, you would identify all of the activities performed be each individual resource and develop a list for each resource. This would provide concise and precise guidance to the resource on what their specific tasks are and when they would be needed.

Resource Name: _____

Activity Start Date	Activity End Date	Activity Description	Seq.#	Interdependent Activity

Sample Activity Registry Worksheet

Project Name: _____

Deliverable:		Activity Seq.#:	
Resources:		Start Date:	
		End Date:	
Cost:	$	Duration:	
Activity Description:			

Deliverable:		Activity Seq.#:	
Resources:		Start Date:	
		End Date:	
Cost:	$	Duration:	
Activity Description:			

Deliverable:		Activity Seq.#:	
Resources:		Start Date:	
		End Date:	
Cost:	$	Duration:	
Activity Description:			

Deliverable:		Activity Seq.#:	
Resources:		Start Date:	
		End Date:	
Cost:	$	Duration:	
Activity Description:			

Deliverable:		Activity Seq.#:	
Resources:		Start Date:	
		End Date:	
Cost:	$	Duration:	
Activity Description:			

Transforming your Life

Project Scheduling Worksheet

Sequential Activities – are activities that have to be completed in a specific order after another activity has been completed. The work is dependent on a previous task.

Concurrent Activities – are activities that can be completed at the same time as other activities by different resources. The tasks are independent to other tasks.

Create a project schedule by placing times and dates to your project activities so that you and your resources know when they need to start working on each activity and how long they should take to complete it and move on to the next activity. The easiest way to begin the process of scheduling your project is to place all of the linear sequential activities in complete order and set aside all activities that can be done concurrent to other activities. The complete linear sequential activity list can then be assigned a start date. When you have selected the start date, you would use each activity duration to schedule the start date of the next, and so on until you have start dates and end dates for every task in sequence, and have identified your project end date as the completion date of your last activity. For the remaining tasks that can be completed concurrent to other activities, you can schedule them at logical times where resources are available to complete the work, keeping in mind any dependencies on other activities in your schedule. You do not want these tasks to cause a delay to others tasks, and if you all your resources are being used, you will want to schedule additional resources to work on these tasks to have them completed in a timely fashion according to your schedule. You can apply this information to a calendar for visual representation of your project schedule.

Seq.#	Activity	Duration	Start Date	End Date	Resources

Project Cost Worksheet

Your activity costs will add up to form your overall project budget, so if you have grouped activities within the initial planning process, you will be able to determine the costs associated to each group of related activities, the costs for each individual resource, material and equipment costs, and more. This information will become valuable if your scope changes or if unforeseen events crop up while your project is running. Budgeting is making sure you have the right amount of money set aside for when you need it. Doing it right means you are prepared and will not delay payments, or worse, run out of money before the project is complete.

Project Name: _____

Seq.#	Activity Description	Cost
1		
2		
3		
4		
~	~~~~~~	~~~~~~~~
28		
29		
30		
	TOTAL COST	

Sample Budget Table

Budget Category	Disbursement 1	Disbursement 2	Disbursement 3	Disbursement 4
Labor				
Services				
Materials				
Facilities				
Computers				
Contingency				
TOTAL				

Resource	Rate	Duration	Total Expenditure
Staff 1	$50.00 per hour	85 hours	$4,250.00
Contractor 1	$1,000.00 per day	12 days	$12,000.00
Contractor 2	$500.00 per day	18 days	$9,000.00
Supplies	$1,000.00 per month	3 months	$3,000.00
Office Space	$2,000.00 per month	3 months	$6,000.00
Computers	$3,000.00 fixed	3 months	$3,000.00
		TOTAL	$37,250.00
Contingency	$10,000.00		

Budget Worksheet

Budget Category	Date ( ) Disbursement 1	Date ( ) Disbursement 2	Date ( ) Disbursement 3	Date ( ) Disbursement 4
TOTAL	$	$	$	$

Expenditure Estimation

Resource	Rate	Duration	Total Expenditure
		TOTAL	$
Contingency			

Resource Management Worksheet

Managing your project resources involves planning when you will need specific resources in your project and lining them up so that they are available at the right time and remain available for the duration of the assigned work. The resources include any and all resources needed to complete the work, whether it be human resources, materials, equipment, capital, or another. Defining the timing of needed resources is vital to minimizing the potential for project delays. Your resource plan is your guide to identifying all the resources needed in your project, and your resource schedule will help you line up your resources to be available at the right times. The next step is deciding how your resources will be managed during project execution.

Resource	Start Date	End Date	Onboarding /Contract Date	Engagement Date	Supervisor

Communication Planning Worksheet

A communication plan provides details about the needs of the various audiences that have a stake in the project. It describes how the project manager, project team and other parties will communicate throughout the course of the project. The first step in developing your communication plan is identifying the people you need to communicate with. Once you know this, you can detail what specific types of information, instruction, or other content you need to relay in your communications and the frequency at which you should provide said details. You should also specify the preferred method of communication such as email, voice, or face to face. Deciding the regularity of team meetings and which team members are required to be present at said meetings would be decided during this step. Requirements for meetings and regular communication with external companies, contractors or other parties can also be reviewed at this stage but are subject to their approval to become a part of your communication plan.

Stakeholder Name	Information Needed	Communication Frequency	Communication Method	Who Provides Info	When Info is Provided

Risk Planning Worksheet

The magic question when trying to envision risks to your projects is "What if?" This question helps form the basis of exploring different scenarios that could take your project into different directions. Because risk is such a broad and all-encompassing array of potentiality, my suggestion to someone new to project management is to start by focusing on the most probable risks and only focus on high and medium level risks (risks that could impact your project by a more than a 25% impact on your iron triangle).

Start assessing risk by looking at events or people that could have a significant impact on your iron triangle and begin identifying high level risks and work your way down to medium and lower level risks. You should not be concerned with every potential risk, rather you want to focus on those highly probably risks. List the Risks and give each a name, determine generally the probability of the risk being realized (high, medium, low) and the potential impact of the risk on your project (large, moderate, small). Then describe the potential impact on your project in detail, prioritize the entire list of project risks, indicate who is responsible for managing the risk if it does happen and finally choose an action that you will take in this event. Typically there are four strategies for managing risks, which include: **accepting** the risk and absorbing impact into your project; **avoiding** the risk by planning around it; **mitigate** the risk again through planning to lessen any potential impact to the project; or, **transfer** the risk to a third party such as an outside resource under contract that would protect your project and leave the potential impact on them.

Risk #	Risk Name	Probability (H/M/L)	Impact (L/M/S) %	Describe Impact	Priority	Person Responsible	Action

Contingency Worksheet

If the magic question to discover if there is a risk to your project is "What if?", then the magic question you need to ask when thinking about contingencies is "What would I do if the risk happens?" A contingency is breathing space that you create in projects to offset potential risks that may affect the iron triangle (Time, Cost, Quality/Performance) or your scope. Variations in these 4 key areas that may come from a risk being realized will impact other areas of your project and each project has unique qualities that must be assessed for the level of risk to the 4 key areas.

From your Risk Worksheet, start with the highest level risks and work your way down. List the risk name, probability (high/medium/low), project impact (large/moderate/small), and impact description. After this is complete, assess which area of your project will be impacted by the risk and determine which constraint will be affected (time/cost/quality/scope). Indicate the affected constraint(s) in the Impact Area column, determine the value of the impact (in time, cost, quality, etc.), and list the value in the Value of Impact column. Finally, set your contingency value and type in the last column for each risk. Working through this process forces you to think critically about your project and plan for events that can negatively impact it. At the end of this process, you should feel empowered in the knowledge that come hell or high water, you are doing everything possible to make this project a success.

Risk Name	Probability (H/M/L)	Impact (L/M/S) %	Impact Description	Impact Area	Value of Impact	Contingency Offset

Problem Management Worksheet

When problems crop up, there are a few steps you can take to work through each problem to effectively address it.

1. Define the problem in detail
2. Identify the affected activities in your project
3. Determine the current and potential impact on other interdependent activities in the project
4. Decide what to do to deal with the problem
   a. Ignore it
   b. Absorb it
   c. Mitigate it
   d. Avoid it
   e. Reduce the impact of it
   f. Transfer it to someone else
   g. Handle it through a combination of the above
5. Check your Iron Triangle to see if you need to make any adjustments

Problem Type	Date Identified	Problem Description	Potential Project Impact	Activities Impacted	Impact on Iron Triangle	Resolution Options	Resolution Chosen	Assigned to Resource

About the Author

With over 20 years of experience working on and managing projects of all sizes and budgets, across many industries Connor Pierce has developed a unique wisdom, sense of humor, ability to successfully deliver projects and transfer the knowledge of project management to just about anyone. Connor's firm belief in the application of project management principles to better an individual's daily life and help them achieve their dreams is based on his own broad experience, and he spends much of his time now delivering this knowledge to people around the world through public and corporate speaking engagements, executive coaching, corporate consulting, and now through this first in a planned series of books intended to help people achieve their dreams in all areas of life.

His passion for learning and seeing others succeed in reaching their life goals is rooted in his own personal journey, leading to his own personal and professional successes. Successful senior professional project manager, executive, entrepreneur, investor, author, public speaker, friend and mentor, Connor applies project management knowledge in his daily life and helps others do the same.

Connor provides a light hearted wealth of knowledge within this book to help readers follow concrete steps to achieve any dream they can imagine. An unconventional self-help book that steps away from traditional high motivation, low useable content, this step by step guide is easy to follow, practical and can be applied over and over throughout a lifetime of bigger and better dreams.

Connor's life has truly been transformed by his wonderful relationship with high-school sweetheart Nancy and two precious children, his best projects to date.